Crystals Healing for Beginners

Discovering the Power of Crystals.
A Beginner's Guide to Crystal Healing
(2023 Crash Course for Beginners)

Celeste Oliver

Contents

Introduction

"Accept whatever the present moment has
to offer as if you had chosen it."

ECKHART TOLLE IS A SPIRITUAL TEACHER.

Congratulations and thank you for purchasing Crystals Healing for Beginners. You are about to embark on a one-of-a-kind mindfulness, healing, and wellness journey.

The chapters that follow will go over crystals and stones and how to incorporate them into your life for a healthier, more positive lifestyle. You will learn how to choose crystals, how to use them in meditation, and which crystals are best for heart, mind, and soul healing and health. This book will teach you how to use crystals to unlock your chakras and will provide information on 100 crystals to use in your health and wellness.

Read about how crystals successfully changed the life of someone else, just like you, and provided the healing that allowed them to become the version of themselves that they desired.

You'll learn the best techniques for cleaning and storing crystals, as well as programming and charging them for daily use. Even with their growing popularity, the uses and applications of crystals for health, healing, and wellness have only scratched the surface of what crystals can do and how they can improve your life.

There are numerous books on this subject available on the market; thank you for selecting this one! Every effort has been made to fill the pages with as much useful information and knowledge as possible. Please enjoy, and remember to read the other books in this series: Chakras Healing for Beginners and Reiki Healing for Beginners.

An Introduction to Crystals and Stones

"Every morning we are reborn. What we
do today is the most important."

-BUDDHA

Crystals and stones are naturally occurring objects that can be found in almost any environment on the planet. But what is it about crystals and stones that make them so special and powerful? For starters, crystals are among the most stable naturally occurring structures on the planet.

A crystalline lattice is a mathematically sound geometric matrix that makes up crystals. The internal lattice of a crystal determines its shape, color, and metaphysical and healing properties. Because of this incredibly stable structure, crystals have a powerful ability to reflect, store, transmute, absorb, and refract various types of energy. This includes both light and heat energy.

Crystals have traditionally been used for a variety of lifestyle enhancements. Crystals were prescribed by healers and physicians in ancient Egypt, Samaria, China, and Mesopotamia to treat mental and physical ailments.

They were meant to be worn or carried, and in some cases ground into a powder and consumed.

Colorful crystals were ground into a fine powder and used in makeup in many ancient societies before more modern methods became available. Crystals and stones have been used in many cultures around the world for jewelry, decoration, and art to add different energetic qualities to a person or a place.

Throughout history, crystals have been used as a source of healing energy and as a way of life.

For thousands of years, including today, Ancient Chinese Medicine, which includes herbal medicine, acupuncture, and crystal medicine, has used crystals as a type of medicine and healing.

Unfortunately, as alchemy and scientific fields of study grew in popularity during the Middle Ages, followed by the modernization of medicine and the emergence of Western medicine, the popularity of 'antiquated' healing practices declined.

It wasn't until the 1970s that crystals became popular again. This popularity has spread and gained traction over the last several decades. Wellness and health are hot topics right now, especially when it comes to holistic health and healing. Many people prefer alternative treatments and therapies to pharmaceuticals and conventional medicine. Organic and natural foods, as well as raw milk and dairy products, are becoming more popular as a form of self-care and wellness. Massage, Reiki energy healing, acupuncture, and crystal therapies are among the fastest-growing fields in the wellness industry.

Crystals offer a one-of-a-kind and natural healing and wellness experience. Every natural item in this world interacts with one another in some way, resulting in an energetic exchange that creates balance. Consider the milkweed plant and the Monarch Caterpillar. Monarch butterflies lay their eggs on milkweed plants. The caterpillars hatch and begin feeding on the leaves. The milkweed secretes a sticky, milky substance as they eat. Approximately one-third of the caterpillars become entangled in the milky substance and die before reaching adulthood.

The caterpillars prune and trim the milkweed plants to keep them from overgrowing, and the milkweed defense mechanism keeps an overpopulation of Monarch Butterflies from reaching maturity. This is a simple example of how natural balance and energy can be found all around you. Having a natural balance and energy is part of what it means to be human. When that energy becomes unbalanced, it does not correct itself.

Looking at the milkweed and the caterpillars again, if milkweed plants began to die in large numbers, there would be insufficient milkweed to feed the monarch caterpillars, causing their population to plummet. On the other hand, if the monarch butterfly population exploded and increased, so would the number of caterpillars, and milkweed plants eliminating one-third of the caterpillars would no longer provide the same balance. As a result, there will be an overpopulation of butterflies and a decrease in milkweed, as well as competition for food for the growing population of monarchs. It is difficult to restore the balance once it has been disrupted.

Internal energetic imbalances in people's bodies are just as common. However, in this modern era, there is a lack of self-awareness, in that people do not always notice when their energy is imbalanced. Disease results from an imbalance of bodily energies. If left unchecked, this state of dis-ease develops into disease, sickness, illness, and even injury. These conditions can manifest as physical, mental, emotional, or spiritual ailments.

Looking at nature and how many natural examples of balance have evolved, it makes sense that there would be natural sources of healing and balance for humans that occur in the world. Crystals are one of the most powerful manifestations of natural healing energy. It is not possible to create or destroy energy, but it can be transformed.

Crystals are invaluable when it comes to changing the energy of your body and life because of their natural ability to absorb, reflect, transmute, refract, and store energy.

Crystal energy cannot always be seen with the naked eye. Not everyone can feel it simply by touching, wearing, or placing a crystal over one of their chakras. Modern science has provided instruments and tools for measuring and viewing the energetic properties of crystals. Thermal energy measuring instruments reveal that many types of crystals emit a heat signature. The same holds true for light energy. The natural color of crystals is an expression of that light energy.

The primary source of power within crystals is energy. What exactly is energy? The textbook definition of energy is "the power derived from the use of chemical or physical sources, particularly to provide heat, light, or power machinery."

Natural energy sources that are commonly used include:

- Thermal (heat)

- Solar (light)

- Wind

- Biomass from Water (wood as fuel)

There are other naturally occurring energy sources. Lightning generates electricity naturally. Everything in the world is infused with energy. Energy, according to the Law of Conservation of Energy, cannot be created or destroyed. Only transformation or transmutation is possible. When you break down the basic components and building blocks of natural structures, you'll notice that they all contain some form of heat, water, light, or another energy source. As a result, they went from an energetic state to a different structure. The same holds true for people.

Heat is produced by the human body. Electrical impulses run through the nervous system of the human body. The human body is composed of 80% water. All of these are significant energetic components.

Returning to crystals, which are powerful energy sources, it is known that energies interact and react with one another. Crystals are an intense, natural source of energy that interacts with the energies of the human body as well as the energies of various objects, materials, and energies in the environment. Crystals can change and influence your body, mind, spirit, and the environment you create for yourself through this interaction and reaction.

Crystals are an amazing natural wonder. They naturally form when a liquid cools and begins to harden. During the cooling process, molecules begin to congregate inside the liquid in an attempt to achieve stability. This process is repeated until the liquid hardens and crystallizes, resulting in a uniform pattern. Cooling magma produces a large number of crystals.

Magma is a source of thermal heat energy and is directly responsible for the formation of numerous crystal types. Temperature, pressure, other elements in the environment, and so on all contribute to the formation of crystals. These variables are responsible for the world's wide variety of crystals.

Variations of each type of crystal, such as quartz, exist. Quartz comes in clear quartz, smoky quartz, amethyst, rose quartz, and a variety of other colors. Jade can be green, red, blue, or a mottled combination of these colors.

Crystals can also be created in a controlled environment. Beautiful artificial crystals have been created in laboratories. While many people believe in the power of artificial crystals, others believe in the power of naturally occurring crystals. This book will concentrate on naturally occurring crystals.

The process by which crystals are formed will have a direct impact on the crystal's crystalline structure. This internal structure is significant because it influences the properties of crystals and what they are best used for.

It is worth noting that the crystalline lattice is not always visible simply by looking at a crystal because the structure is on an internal molecular level and does not always carry over to the external shape of the crystal.

If you are new to working with crystals, you may be unable to determine the internal crystalline structure if you have no prior knowledge of it. However, as you continue to work with crystals and develop your intuition, you will be able to identify crystal properties and structures. In your crystal studies and as you begin to use crystals to enhance and change your life, your intuition will be a valuable tool.

There are six different crystal structures:

- Cubic

- Hexagonal

- Monoclinic

- Orthorhombic

- Tetragonal

- Triclinic

The Cubic Structure (Amplifiers)

Cubic crystals are designed to ground and stabilize energy. They also work to relieve tension and cleanse the body. The cubic crystals' isometric (cubic) crystalline structure improves situations. These crystals have harmonic symmetry and are frequently used to improve health, wealth, and other aspects of the body, mind, and life.

Amplifiers are commonly used to improve situations, which is why they are called such.

Fluorite, garnet, halite, lapis lazuli, pyrite, and spinel are some popular cubic crystals.

Hexagonal Design (Explorers)

Hexagonal Structure Crystals provide support while also organizing and balancing energy. The external structure of many hexagonal crystals mirrors the internal crystalline lattice. This manifests as a pointed crystal that resembles an arrowhead. Hexagonal crystals are good for providing focus and direction, especially when looking for new opportunities. That is why they are referred to as explorers or seekers. They can illuminate your path.

Hexagonal crystals are best known for their ability to help you achieve your goals. They can act as a compass on a new venture or when you embark on a new path and help guide you to success. These ventures or paths can be motivated by love, career choices, or actual travel adventures, among other things.

Agates, aquamarine, calcite, emerald, morganite, tourmaline, and quartz are examples of hexagonal crystals (amethyst, clear, citrine).

Structures that are monoclinic (Protectors)

When the focus is physical, this structure group's crystals are used. They are thought to improve perception and purify the body. These crystals are known as guardians, and they work best with physical objects like possessions, a home, or the physical body. They provide a strong shield of safety and protection.

The monoclinic crystals' crystalline structure is made up of several parallelograms. This structure gives these crystals a resonance that is used to protect and safeguard them on both a physical and spiritual level. They are also known to assist people in remaining true to their path and beliefs. These shields are best used as precautions.

Azurite, diopside, gypsum, howlite, jade, malachite, mica, and selenite are examples of monoclinic crystals.

Structures that are orthorhombic (Releasers)

Crystals with an orthorhombic structure aid in the flow of information and energy. They are known as releasers because they focus on clearing and cleansing energy. Orthorhombic crystals are the best choice for releasing energy or imbalances on a physical, emotional, mental, or energetic level.

These crystals not only emit dissonant energy, but they also aid in energy realignment. They restore resonant energy to the body, place, or object. Imbalances can manifest as pain, disease, grief, worry, fear, and so on. Orthorhombic crystals are extremely beneficial in resolving a wide range of imbalances.

Orthorhombic crystals have a diamond-shaped crystalline structure. This shape encourages energy to flow outwards, allowing it to be released.

Angel site, aragonite, barite, bronzite, chrysocolla, peridot, and topaz are examples of orthorhombic crystals.

Tetragonal Design (Charmers)

Tetragonal crystals aid in the resolution of issues and situations. They open and balance energy in the vicinity of intentions. The tetragonal crystalline structure frequently imparts a gleaming sheen to the crystal's exterior. This sheen is usually pleasing to the eye and draws attention. Hexagonal crystals and tetragonal crystals complement hexagonal crystals well. They can work together to help you seek and attract your desires.

They are known as charmers because they enhance the power of other crystals in your life and for healing. They can also be used to improve the appearance of someone or something.

Not just physically appealing, and not just romantically interesting. Tetragonal crystals, in general, work best when combined with the power of other crystals.

Chalcopyrite, rutile, rutilated quartz, and vesuvianite are examples of tetragonal crystals.

Structure with three peaks (Perimeters)

Crystals from the triclinic group enhance perception. They aid in the discovery of new dimensions. These crystals are especially powerful. They are excellent for both protection and seeing through illusions. Monoclinic crystals are used to protect valuable items. Tetragonal crystals are oriented outward. They keep outward dissonant energies from attracting you.

A trapezium is formed by the internal lattice of triclinic crystals. This lattice shaping gives these crystals strength in all directions. They are called perimeters because they protect you or other objects from unwanted energies. They are transformed into wards of protection.

Amazonite, kyanite, labradorite, moonstone, sunstone, and ulexite are some well-known triclinic crystals.

Some stones and gems with resonant energetic properties do not have a crystalline lattice. These are referred to as amorphous solids. They don't have the geometric stability of real crystals, but they're still energetic and can be used for balancing, healing, and lifestyle changes.

Jet, obsidian, opal, and pearl are examples of amorphous solids.

Amorphous solids, while lacking the solid mathematical properties of true crystals, are no less energetically powerful.

There are other properties of crystals that will contribute to their use in healing and working with their energy.

Color is a component of crystal makeup that influences how a crystal can be used. The color of a crystal is determined in part by its crystalline lattice, but also by the conditions under which it is formed. Light is reflected in color. Light is an energy source. Crystals absorb, transmute, and refract energy, including light, and this is how they get their color.

Different colors have different energies that you can use with crystals to help you change and balance your life.

Red crystals have metaphysical and balancing properties associated with power, energy, and passion. These ideas can be further refined to include strength, desire, and heat. Red has long been associated with love, aggression, danger, the element fire, and blood. It is also associated with intensity, luck, celebration, and putting an end to the danger.

These characteristics are not unique to red crystals. Red crystals can also have properties that are distinct from those associated with their color. Knowing a crystal's color properties, on the other hand, is a good place to start.

Garnet, red jasper, red jade, and ruby are examples of common red crystals.

Yellow

Yellow is most commonly associated with happiness, joy, and sunshine. It can also be associated with both danger and optimism. The color yellow is associated with hope and philosophy. Deception, dishonesty, cowardice, and betrayal are also prohibited.

The majority of color associations have both positive and negative connotations. This improves their ability to balance energies.

Citrine, sunstone, and tiger's eye are well-known yellow crystals.

Green

Nature's color is green. It is also the color of health and the environment. Green represents fortune, abundance, finances and money, and youth. It is also linked to envy, jealousy, inexperience, and fertility.

Green is another extremely versatile color that can be used to address a wide range of energetic requirements. Green crystals' environmental association makes them a good candidate for balancing energies in your personal environment, such as a house or a specific room in a house, or even a work environment. Green is associated with the earth element.

Aventurine, emerald, jade, malachite, moldavite, and peridot are some common green crystals.

Blue is an intriguing color because different shades of blue can have different energetic properties. Dark blue and light blue can have distinct meanings. Blue is commonly associated with peace, harmony, unity, trust, and truth.

Blue's other energetic properties include confidence, security, conversation, and communication. Blue is also associated with cleanliness, depression, loyalty, protection, and stability. It is also linked to the element of water and the sky.

Blue lace agate, blue topaz, lapis lazuli, and sapphire are some well-known blue crystals.

Purple

Purple, like blue, can have different energetic properties depending on its hue. Indigo and violet are common purple shades associated with the chakras. A later chapter will go over the differences between indigo and violet.

Purple crystals are still associated with some generic energetic associations. Spirituality, mystery, and transformation are among the associations. Purple is also associated with royalty or nobility. Purple is associated with enlightenment and wisdom.

Amethyst, lepidolite, and fluorite are some well-known purple crystals.

Orange

Orange, like red, is a color of warmth. However, the properties of the orange vary. The properties of the orange color include energy, vitality, and enthusiasm. Orange is also associated with balance, which is important in energy work. The color orange is associated with growth and flamboyance.

Amber, calcite, and carnelian are examples of well-known orange crystals.

Gray

There are gray crystals out there, believe it or not. Some of these crystals are quite common and can be very beneficial in energy work and energy balancing.

Gray is most commonly associated with safety and dependability. It is also associated with wisdom, modesty, and maturity. Gray is associated with melancholy feelings, old age, and intense grief.

Hematite and smoky quartz are two commonly known gray crystals.

Brown

Brown is another earth-toned color associated with trees. Brown is most closely associated with home, hearth, and comfort. Brown is associated with endurance, stability, nature, simplicity, and dependability.

Bronzite, pyrite, shiva lingam, and tiger's eye are some brown crystals used in energy work and balancing.

White

Clear crystals, which are used in crystal healing, are also classified as white crystals. White represents purity and virginity. It is also linked to purity, peace, humility, and innocence. White is traditionally associated with matrimony and marriage, as well as birth and youth.

Cryolite, moonstone, opal, selenite, and clear quartz are all common white and clear crystals.

Black

The perception of black as a negative color is not entirely correct. Colors have both positive and negative connotations. Black, on the other hand, is frequently perceived as a dark, negative, and depressing color. Black is merely a color. Because it is a dark color, it is not inherently negative.

Indeed, black is a powerful protective color that is also associated with elegance, power, and depth. It has been linked to sadness, depression, grief, and fear. Everyone experiences these emotions. Black crystals can assist in balancing strong, unwanted emotions.

In addition, black is associated with wealth, mystery, and formality.

Apache tear, black tourmaline, jet, obsidian, onyx, and Tibetan black quartz are all common black crystals.

When considering the properties of a crystal, color is an important consideration. Of course, not all crystals are the same color. Some crystals exhibit a variety of colors.

Bloodstone, howlite, mookaite jasper, tree agate, and watermelon tourmaline are a few examples of multi-colored crystals.

Color properties of all the colors present in multicolored crystals are frequently present. These crystals are excellent for balancing multiple chakras at once or addressing multiple layers of an energetic imbalance.

When it comes to the healing and balancing energetic properties of your crystals, color, and crystalline structure are both important considerations. Of course, not every crystal matches the color or structure properties exactly.

Crystals and stones have long been used in human society for healing, spiritual and religious practices, ceremonies, fashion, medicine, and a variety of other purposes. Getting into crystal wellness and energy is becoming much easier now that they are gaining popularity and there is renewed interest in crystals and their uses.

The world of crystals is vast, and this crystals and healing guide will give you everything you need to get started. Choose crystals and their distinct and impressive energy as a wellness, healing, and lifestyle option to change and balance the energy within yourself, your surroundings, and the aspects of your life that you wish to change.

The Fundamentals of Crystal Healing

"Which day is it?" Pooh inquired.
'It's today,' Piglet said.
'My favorite day,' Pooh said."

The power of crystals has been well documented throughout history and in modern techniques. Crystals are a powerful source of natural energetic power that, when combined with other energies, can heal and balance.

Energy can take many forms. Thermal heat energy, solar light energy, hydropower water energy, wind energy, lightning as electrical energy and biomass energy as a fuel source have all been discussed previously.

There are other types of natural energies. Sound is converted into waves, which are energetic pulses. Movement converts body fuels to energy. There are two types of energy: kinetic energy, which is the energy of movement, and potential energy, which is energy that has the potential to become kinetic energy.

Everything in the universe is made up of matter and energy, including crystals and people. Every form of matter vibrates energetically. The vibratory frequency of an object or being is determined by the type of energy it possesses. This vibration is converted into a frequency that is broadcast into the environment. The concept of putting what you want out into the world is based on expressing an energetic frequency in order to gain a personal desire.

When your energetic matter is operating at the desired or ideal frequency, your body, mind, emotions, and spirit should be healthy and free of disease.

Dis-ease manifests in the body when you are resonating at an imbalanced frequency or when your personal vibration is off.

Many factors can cause energetic vibrations to become unbalanced. Perhaps you have a physical or emotional trauma that has yet to be resolved. Perhaps you work at a desk and spend all day sitting in the same position, causing improper energy flow through the body. Perhaps you work at a job that is completely unsatisfying and you feel like your life is a series of shades of gray with no satisfaction.

The majority of imbalances are caused by blocked or overactive energy, resulting in a shift in your personal vibration and energetic frequency. They can be the result of an emotional, physical, or spiritual disturbance in your life.

Crystals can be used to realign personal energetic frequencies because they are so effective at absorbing, transmuting, storing, refracting, and transforming energy. Crystals absorb excess energy, transform blocks, and release trapped energy.

While most blockages and overactive energetic vibrations appear to be negative, this is not always the case. An energetic frequency can become overactive but not always in such an obvious way. Energy imbalances can cause hyperactivity, excessive talkativeness, overconfidence, and arrogance.

While these symptoms and representations of the disease may not be as severe as physical pain or illness, they can be disruptive to daily life. Even when daily life is disrupted, these overactive imbalances can benefit from realignment.

What does it feel like to have your energy aligned and operating at an optimal frequency?

The answer to this question will be determined by a number of factors. The length of time your energy has been imbalanced is a major factor. The longer an imbalance is allowed to persist, the lower your vibration becomes. It can not only affect the areas where and how your energy is imbalanced, but it can also cause additional imbalances in your body.

Consider the energy flowing through your body as a series of pools connected by a stream. If one pool begins to overflow, the stream between pools becomes faster, raising the water level in the other pools and causing more overflow.

If one of the pools becomes clogged with leaves and grass, it will begin to back up into itself. When this happens, the pools below the blockage do not receive the same amount of water and begin to dry up.

Energy in the body operates in a similar manner. The longer an imbalance persists, the more impact it has on the body and other energetic currents.

As a result, when the body is in perfect balance, it is free of chronic pain and physical aches and pains. When the body is balanced, it experiences an overall state of health and wellness. This is about more than just physical health and wellness. This includes emotional and spiritual well-being.

A healthy, positive emotional and thought process results from a balanced energetic flow. Depression, anxiety, low self-esteem, or a pessimistic outlook will not befall someone with a balanced energetic vibration.

People with balanced energy are more likely to pursue their own passions and find success and fulfillment in most aspects of life. That expression of love in which reds appear redder, flowers smell prettier, and chocolate tastes sweeter, can also be applied to an energetically balanced vibration.

Furthermore, when your vibration is balanced and your frequency is aligned, you begin to attract people, situations, jobs, friends, romantic partners, and other aspects of your life and environment that resonate best with her aligned frequency. Such energetic connections only add to the fulfillment and satisfaction of living a balanced and healthy lifestyle.

When the energetic flow in the body is operating at its peak vibration, the human body and mind can easily maintain optimal health and wellness. The use of natural energy-balancing methods, such as crystals, will help the body learn how to heal itself in the future.

Crystal healing can be either intense or subtle. When your energies connect with a crystal and begin to find balance, you may notice it immediately. You may experience a powerful emotional release in the form of tears or a physical release in the form of trembling. Sometimes the outcomes are more subtle, with no obvious release or indication that the energy imbalances have been corrected.

Your intuition can help guide you through the more subtle energetic shifts when the crystals' work is complete. It is critical to cleanse your crystals before reusing them. A later chapter will go into greater detail about how to cleanse your crystals to keep them primed for energetic healing.

Crystals can be used in a variety of ways to help restore balance. Some are very simple, while others evolve into more complex rituals.

Crystals are commonly used in the following ways:

- Carrying or wearing a crystal

- Setting up a crystal grid

- Elixirs of crystal

- Incorporating crystals into meditation

- Using a crystal to adorn your body

- Crystal Programming

Additional chapters will go over programming crystals, meditation with crystals, and using crystals to align the chakras in greater detail.

The following crystal energy methods work on both the body and the environment to balance internal and external energy sources.

Wearing or transporting crystals

Many crystals are small enough to fit in a pocket, backpack, purse, or wallet. Carrying a crystal around allows the crystal's energies to bond with you and your systems. As a result, it begins to work.

Having the crystal close by will allow it to work with your personal energies, whether that work is to absorb energy or release blocks. Over time, you may discover that you no longer feel the need to carry that crystal with you, or that the feelings that prompted you to begin carrying that crystal no longer interfere with your daily life.

Wearing crystals is the same. Many crystals are fashioned into jewelry, such as rings, necklace pendants, bracelets, wire wraps, and so on. Because jewelry frequently comes into direct contact with your skin, the crystal is in closer proximity to your energy.

Some stones are more difficult to find pre-made into jewelry. Necklaces and bracelets with a wire basket or locket-like pendants designed to hold a small crystal that can be swapped out whenever you feel the need for a change can be purchased.

Crystals and gemstones can be lovely and make an excellent accented fashion accessory. However, not everyone enjoys wearing jewelry. Jewelry made with crystals can be quite expensive. A portion of that cost may be attributed to the polishing and cutting of crystals. This process does not necessarily increase the potency of the crystals.

Raw crystals are just as energetically potent as polished crystals, if not more so because they haven't been altered in any way. Cutting, polishing, and modifying a crystal can alter its energetic frequencies. That is not to say that it will deplete its energetic properties.

Carrying crystals or wearing crystal jewelry is a very hands-off, passive method of using crystals for healing. It doesn't take much conscious effort to remember to put on your jewelry or tuck the crystals into your pockets or purse every morning.

Putting a Crystal on Your Body

Placing a crystal on your body to heal yourself energetically is a method that has been practiced for centuries.

A common headache treatment is to lie flat and comfortably on your back, with a clear quartz point facing up towards the top of your head. Close your eyes and feel the energy of the crystal soak into you. This procedure is intended to allow the crystal's energy to balance the energy in your mind and relieve the headache.

This is a simple example of placing a crystal on your body to realign and balance energies.

Placing crystals directly on the body can relieve and balance ailments in both the physical and energetic bodies.

Choosing crystals that correspond to each chakra and then placing them on the chakra location on your body and allowing yourself to relax with those crystals is a great way to work towards chakra balance by placing crystals on the body.

This method of crystal healing does necessitate some relaxation and allowing yourself enough time to absorb the crystal's energies. When using crystals on the body, there are a few things to keep in mind.

Crystals come in a variety of shapes, including tumbled stones, crystal points, clusters, wands, and so on. Depending on the shape of the crystal, you may need to position it on your body differently. Furthermore, some crystals work best when placed on specific parts of the body. Even if the goal is to balance energy in a different area of the body, certain organs can assist in activating crystals' energetic properties.

It is important to remember that some crystals are slightly radioactive or contain toxic elements when placed directly on your skin or worn as jewelry. Allowing them to come into direct contact with the skin for extended periods of time can be problematic. It is recommended that you learn about possible toxicity levels before using crystals on your skin or wearing them close to your body, or consult a professionally trained crystal master.

Making a Crystal Grid Work

Crystal grids are a powerful healing tool that can become quite complex when used in many different healing and energy modalities. If you decide to use a crystal grid, your intuition will be your most valuable tool in building and activating your crystal grid.

A crystal grid is a geometric arrangement of crystals that have been activated for healing or balancing purposes. Geometric shapes are used in the construction of crystal grids because different shapes correspond to different energetic healing properties.

You'll be relying heavily on your intuition as you choose crystals for your crystal grid. Close your eyes and place your hands over your crystal collection if you're still working on your intuition. If your fingers brush against any of the crystals or your palms begin to warm when hovering over a specific crystal, it is a good indication that you should include that crystal in your grid.

You may discover that the geometric shape of your grid is also constructed intuitively rather than preplanned. When it comes to crystal grids, you don't always need a detailed plan. While working with crystals, this will be one of your most intuitive healing methods.

When you decide to use a crystal grid, make sure you have enough time and private space to construct and then activate your crystal grid. It is a form of therapeutic healing, and a session, even if performed on yourself, can take a long time, sometimes up to an hour or more if you are completely immersed in the energy.

If you can sit in a comfortable chair or lie on a bed or massage table while using a crystal grid, you can build the grid underneath the chair, bed, or table. If you don't have the option of using one of those methods, putting the grid as close to where you'll be as possible is ideal.

Because a crystal grid healing session can take some time, making the environment more comfortable with dim lighting, relaxing music, or even burning incense is a good way to increase your ability to absorb the crystal healing energy. When your body and mind are relaxed, they are in their optimal state for healing and recovery.

After you've established your healing environment and chosen the crystals for your grid, it's time to build the grid. You will possess a master crystal. This crystal will serve as the grid's focal point. It could be placed in the grid's center or at the top, depending on where your intuition tells you the focal point of your geometric shape is.

The rest of the crystals that you place in your grid will be placed one at a time. You'll begin in the center and work your way out. After you've built the grid, you'll want to activate it by closing your eyes and focusing on the intention of the healing session.

When you feel the grid has been activated, get comfortable by lying down or sitting and soaking up the energy. While the crystal grid energy is active, you may begin to feel different sensations as you relax.

During a crystal grid healing session, you may experience physical sensations such as warmth or tingling. You may experience a humming sensation on your skin or relief from physical pain.

During a crystal grid healing session, you may experience emotional sensations. You may burst out laughing, cry, or become extremely angry! If emotions arise during a healing session, you should fully feel and release them because the crystals are drawing them out of you.

Other experiences, such as visions or altered states of consciousness, are possible. You might smell, hear, taste, or feel something that isn't physically present.

You should relax during the healing session for as long as you feel necessary. A crystal grid healing can take as little as ten minutes. Other times, you'll need to soak in the crystal energy for a longer period of time.

Allow yourself some time to reconnect to your skin after you feel you have received the healing you require from the grid. To help you ground yourself, sit or stand slowly and drink a glass of cool water. After a crystal grid healing session, it is common to feel energized or rejuvenated. It is also common to feel dizzy or lightheaded following a session. Another grounding exercise is to place your palms or forehead on the ground and breathe into it to feel connected to it.

Everyone has a unique experience with the power of crystals and crystal healing. It may be beneficial to keep a journal of your crystal grid session experiences. Keeping track of what you sense, feel, and she can assist you in determining how the crystal energy is affecting your life and health. Particularly if the changes are more subtle. Keeping track of any changes, no matter how subtle, will assist you in tracking your own progress.

Crystal grids can also be used to heal others. If you intend to provide healing services to others, it is a good idea to have a designated healing space. During a session, you'll want your clients to feel at ease and relaxed. You'll want to make sure they understand what crystal healing is and what sensations and experiences they might have.

Remember that everyone experiences crystal energy differently. If your clients report any other experiences that they have never had or are unfamiliar with, keep in mind that everyone experiences crystal energy differently. As a healer, you are there to provide compassion and healing to your clients, not to tell them that what they are experiencing is incorrect.

When working with clients, you should definitely take notes on what they report to you as well as why they came to see you. You'll need to establish trust with your clients and understand that if they're coming to you for crystal healing sessions, they may have already had negative experiences with conventional doctors.

You will be offering a valuable healing and wellness service. Compassion, sympathy, and empathy will help you connect with your clients and establish trust.

Crystals are an excellent tool for improving your own life, but you can also use them to help others if they are willing and interested in the services you offer.

Elixirs of Crystal

A crystal elixir is a water that has been imprinted with a specific crystal's vibrational energy. Once the crystal has been imprinted on the water, it can be used medicinally in appropriate dose concentrations.

There are two methods for making a crystal elixir, and the method you use will be determined by the crystal you are using.

The Direct Immersion method involves immersing a crystal in water to imprint the liquid.

The Indirect Immersion method involves placing a barrier between the crystal and the water, such as plastic or glass, to prevent direct contact between the crystal and the water.

If you're making an elixir with a crystal that contains trace amounts of radioactivity or toxic elements, the indirect imprint method is ideal. Some crystals, such as selenite, are known to dissolve in water, so you wouldn't want to leave one in direct contact with water for an extended period of time.

To make a crystal elixir, you must first determine your goal or intention for the elixir. Is it going to be the kind you ingest or the kind you apply topically? Crystal elixirs can be used for either purpose.

Once you've determined your elixir's goal, you can select your crystal or crystals. An elixir is not restricted to a single crystal. The imprint of multiple crystals can increase the potency. It is possible, however, to over-energize an elixir. Crystals contain a lot of energy, and sometimes less is more. Too many competing or diverging energies can detract from the main goal or focus.

After you've collected your crystals, fill a clear glass bowl with filtered or purified water. Spring water is also an option, but mineral water is not.

Next, place your crystals in the bowl of water, or place them on the plastic or glass barrier before placing the barrier in the water. The bowl should then be placed in the sun. You can leave it outside in the sun, but if you do, cover the bowl with a mesh covering, such as cheesecloth, to prevent debris from falling in.

You can also place the bowl in a window that receives several hours of direct sunlight per day. Although direct sunlight is preferred, both methods are effective.

The elixir should be exposed to sunlight for at least four hours to fully imprint the energetic vibration of the crystals.

Once your crystal elixir has been imprinted, transfer it to a glass bottle with a dropper. You should store the elixir in an amber or blue glass bottle. When you first start using the elixir, make sure to follow the dosage instructions. The energy vibrations of the crystals used in the elixirs are used to make these dose recommendations. Crystals have three vibrational states: high, calming, and normal energetic.

To use an elixir internally, mix a few drops into a glass of water and drink it, following the dosage recommendations below.

Internal Application

Add 4 drops to every 8 ounces of water for High Energy crystal elixirs. This treatment should be used twice a day for 7 to 14 days.

Mix 3 to 4 drops of the elixir into every 8 ounces of water when using Normal Energy crystals. Continue using this remedy 3–4 times per day for up to 30 days.

The recommended dose for Calming Energy crystal elixirs is 6 to 8 drops mixed with every 8 ounces of water. This elixir can be taken three to four times per day, as needed.

For external use, you'll need a glass spray bottle to dilute your elixir with water before spraying it directly onto the affected area.

External Application

Mix 6 to 8 drops of High Energy crystal elixir per tablespoon of water in your spray bottle. Apply twice a day.

In your spray bottle, combine 8 to 10 drops of elixir per tablespoon of water to make a Normal Energy crystal elixir. You are only allowed to use one application per day.

With Calming Energy crystal elixirs, mix 1 drop per 1 tablespoon of water in your spray bottle. To use, apply a single application as needed but keep it to a minimum.

Elixirs can supplement other crystal healing methods such as crystal grids or sessions in which you lay crystals on your own or another person's body. Elixirs can also be used in conjunction with other healing methods. They are powerful, if not subtler, and make excellent enhancers.

Using an elixir in conjunction with Reiki or Massage can greatly enhance the session.

CHAPTER 3

Crystals and Chakras

"Nature moves slowly, but everything gets done."

– LAO TZU

The Chakra system is one of the body's most well-known energetic systems. Chakras are energy centers in the body. The chakras promote a healthy energy flow through the body cavities, to all organs and systems.

In the body, there are seven main chakras and several sub-chakras. The seven major chakras are located along the spine. They correspond to physical cavities and organs in the body, as well as emotions. Because all chakras are connected, when one is blocked or imbalanced, it causes widespread dis-ease in the body. When one chakra is out of balance, the flow of energy in the other chakras is disrupted.

The Crown Chakra, Third Eye Chakra, Throat Chakra, Heart Chakra, Solar Plexus Chakra, Sacral Chakra, and Root Chakra are the seven major chakras.

Some of the body's sub-chakras can be found in the palms, just below the feet, above the crown chakra, and above the heart chakra. Sub chakras are smaller energy pools in the body that connect to the main chakra system.

The chakras serve as a link between the electromagnetic and physical bodies. The chakras are also connected to other energetic bodies like the auras. This chapter will primarily cover the seven major chakras.

Chakras are cone-shaped energy centers. The point of the cone connects to the spine for the sacral, solar plexus, heart, throat, and third eye chakras. The cone expands outwards to the front and back of the body.

The crown and root chakras each have a cone point that is rooted in the spine. The crown chakra rises from the top of the head, while the root chakra falls from the base of the spine.

The energy within the chakras spirals in a clockwise direction. The energy rotates both clockwise and counterclockwise.

Because the chakras are such an important link between the physical and energetic bodies, an imbalance can significantly disrupt the overall flow of health and wellness within the body. Balancing the chakras is one of the most important processes in maintaining health and wellness for long-term body function.

Because each chakra is an energetic center, and crystals are strong energetic conduits, crystals resonate strongly with the chakras. Crystals can be used to cleanse, activate, or align/balance the chakras. Energy imbalances can manifest themselves as either under activity and blockages or overactivity and overflow. A chakra can be stimulated or sedated by crystals.

Color, crystals, physical, and emotional associations are associated with each chakra. These associations determine which chakras require attention. A blocked crown chakra, for example, can cause chronic nightmares. If you or a client has frequent nightmares, you should consider working on balancing the crown chakra to alleviate nightmares.

The chakras are located in various body cavities known as Chakra Cavities. Each cavity contains organs and glands that are linked to the chakra that rules over it. The reproductive cavity and system, which include male and female reproductive organs, are linked to the Root Chakra. Women who experience severe menstrual pain may benefit from balancing the Root Chakra, which is linked to the reproductive organs and cycles.

As you learn more about the chakras and their associations, you'll be able to independently link emotional and physical ailments back to the chakras and know which chakras need to be balanced to relieve symptoms and heal the body, mind, and spirit.

Chakra of the Root

The root chakra, also known as the base chakra, can be found at the base of the spine. It leaves the spine at the base, pointing down towards the feet. It is wrapped around the coccyx or tailbone. The pelvic cavity is the root chakra cavity. It is linked to both men's and women's reproductive organs, as well as the reproductive glands of the ovaries and testes. The root chakra is associated with reproductive and sexual hormones, as well as development.

Survival and security are emotional and metaphysical connections to the root chakra, which is associated with the element earth. It establishes the foundation for your being and personality. The root chakra is red in color. It is associated with the sensation of being grounded.

Dancing, jogging, and jumping are all good ways to keep this chakra healthy. The root chakra's message to the body is 'I Exist.'

Obesity, hemorrhoids, foot problems, constipation, and leg, blood, and bone problems can all occur when the body is out of balance. The body is tired, the mind is anxious, and there are survival issues. Libido can be reduced.

Physical energy levels, groundedness, fitness, and practicality are all improved by crystal healing the root chakra.

Garnet, ruby, smoky quartz, black tourmaline, and obsidian are all crystals that can be used to heal the root chakra.

Chakra Sacral

The sacral chakra, also known as the 2nd chakra, is located in the front of the body about two or three inches below the navel. It's right on the sacrum, the flat part of the lower back, in the back of the body. The sacral chakra is linked to the abdominal-pelvic cavity. It is associated with the adrenal glands, the immune system, and lower abdominal organs such as the bladder and uterine tract.

The sacral chakra is orange in color. It's linked to sensuality, pleasure, and sexuality. Water is the element associated with the sacral chakra. This is the hub of your interests and dreams. Belly dancing, yoga, and having a loving relationship will help to keep the sacral chakra balanced and functioning.

The sacral chakra sends you the message 'I Desire.'

When the sacral chakra is out of balance, it can cause boredom, disdain, over-seriousness, resentment, clinging to the past, and bladder and uterine disorders. Imbalances can also cause sexual dysfunction, a lack of desire, and erectile dysfunction.

Healing the sacral chakra with crystals improves creativity, enjoyment, curiosity, exploration, pleasure, sensuality, and dynamism.

Carnelian, copper, red jasper, and amber are crystals that can be used to balance and heal the sacral chakra.

Chakra of the Solar Plexus

The solar plexus chakra, also known as the third chakra, is located in the front of the body, an inch or two above the naval, and about three inches above the sacrum in the back. It is linked to the abdominal cavity and digestive system organs such as the stomach and intestines. It is also linked to the pancreas and regulates metabolism-related hormones.

The solar plexus chakra governs personal power. It's also the home of the inner child. The solar plexus chakra is yellow and associated with the element of fire. The term "fire in your belly" refers to the solar plexus chakra. Obsessive-compulsive behavior can result from an overactive chakra.

When balanced, you will have a strong sense of being in control of your own destiny and following your own dreams. The message from the solar plexus chakra is 'I Control.'

When the solar plexus chakra is out of balance, it can cause fatigue, poor decision-making skills, and immune and nervous system issues.

Crystal energy that balances the solar plexus chakras increases personal power, self-reliance, assuredness, joy, better digestion, integrity, and self-confidence.

Citrine, yellow topaz, pyrite, and tiger's eye are some of the most common crystals used to balance the solar plexus chakra.

Chakra of the Heart

The heart chakra is located in the center of the front of the chest, at the base of the sternum. The heart chakra is located on the spine between the lower corners of the shoulder blades in the back. It aligns with the diaphragm that separates the abdominal and thoracic cavities. The heart chakra is connected to the thymus gland, lymphatic system, heart organ, diaphragm, and lungs.

Green is the color associated with the heart chakra. Pink is also associated with the heart chakra, but specifically with the sub-chakra above the heart. The heart chakra is associated with love and compassion on an emotional level. It is the center of the heart and corresponds to the element of air.

Foster healthy relationships with friends, family, romantic partners, and pets to keep the heart chakra healthy. Another good way to keep the heart chakra healthy is to find appreciation and beauty in nature. On a cosmic scale, be open to receiving and giving love.

'I Love' is the message that the heart chakra has for you.

When the heart chakra is out of balance, it causes a lack of self-confidence. It has the potential to lead to self-destructive behavior and tendencies. Fear can also result from an imbalanced heart chakra.

When the heart chakra is properly balanced, it promotes healthy relationships. It encourages empathy and harmony. It promotes balance and love in your life as well as in your surroundings.

Emerald, moldavite, malachite, rose quartz, rhodonite, and morganite are common crystals that can balance the heart chakra.

Chakra of the Throat

The throat chakra is located in the front at the base of the throat and in the back at the center of the spine just above the shoulder blades. It connects to the thoracic cavity. The thyroid gland is linked to the throat chakra. It controls the body's temperature and metabolism. It is also connected to the esophagus, vocal cords, mouth, tongue, and larynx, as well as other thoracic cavity organs.

The throat chakra governs both verbal and subtle communication. It is where you speak your truth and where you keep your truth. The throat chakra is blue in color. When it is working properly, you have the ability to request what you require. By communicating, this chakra reflects your truth in the world. Singing, breathing exercises, and chanting help to keep the throat chakra balanced and healthy.

The throat chakra sends you the message 'I Express.' Do not hide your truth. Speak the truth. Sing the truth.

A stiff neck is one of the symptoms of an imbalanced throat chakra. Imbalances can cause sore throats as well as thyroid issues. An imbalanced throat chakra can also cause problems with the ears and hearing.

When the throat chakra is worked on with crystals and balanced, it aids in communication and expression. It also promotes peace, understanding, and genuine communication.

Blue lace agate and celestite are two crystals that can be used to balance the throat chakra.

Chakra of the Third Eye

The third eye chakra is located in the front of the brow, between the brows. The third eye chakra is located at the occiput on the back of the body. The third eye chakra governs the cranial cavity, is linked to the pituitary gland and regulates hormone production. It communicates with the eyes, ears, and nose.

The chakra of the third eye is the seat of intuition and insight. This third eye chakra is associated with awareness and guidance. Meditation and visualization exercises promote a balanced energy flow, which helps to keep the third eye chakra healthy. The third eye chakra sends you the message, 'I am the Witness.' Indigo is the color associated with the third eye chakra.

Depression, mental and emotional turmoil and anguish are all symptoms of third eye chakra imbalances.

When the third eye chakra is balanced, it improves perception, comprehension, vision, intuition, and perspective. A balanced third eye chakra can also help you become more aware of your surroundings. It can also improve psychic abilities.

Crystals associated with the third eye chakra and capable of balancing it include iolite, lapis lazuli, kyanite, and azurite.

Chakra of the Crown

The crown chakra is at the very top of the head. It reaches all the way to the universe and connects all energies. The crown chakra is linked to the brain, the pineal gland, and the spirit. It controls biological cycles as well as sleep.

The crown chakra is associated with the color violet or even clear and represents spiritual connection. It represents the space between the physical and the spiritual. The crown chakra represents bliss, unity, and the knowledge of being one with all. This chakra is associated with cosmic consciousness and peace. The message you receive from this chakra is 'I am that I am.' Meditation and Reiki are excellent tools for maintaining the crown chakra's balance.

When the crown chakra is out of balance, it causes nightmares, headaches, and vision problems. It can also cause a schism between the physical and spiritual bodies. Spiritual issues can also arise.

When the crown chakra is balanced, it promotes integration into life and self, as well as a sense of belonging, coherence, and spiritual ease. Spirituality and connection to the universe are enhanced when the crown chakra is balanced. This connection extends beyond connecting to the universe and includes connecting to everything, including other people, animals, nature, the elements, and so on.

Amethyst, clear quartz, tanzanite, charoite, and sugilite are crystals that can be used to balance the crown chakra.

When you talk to clients and consider your own behaviors, thought patterns, and any physical symptoms that are expressed or present, you should be able to begin relating them back to specific chakras. Chakras correspond to body cavities, organs, glands, body systems, and emotional connections.

Humans have a physical body, emotions, hormones, and a spiritual body. The chakras are the centers that connect the various aspects of the human body, resulting in unity, harmony, and balance.

These chakras' health and proper function are critical for optimal health and wellness. This isn't just about physical health and wellness. If you are working in an unsatisfying job, you may become stuck in the pattern and believe that you have no other options. Your chakras may become blocked and out of balance. This only adds to the sense of being stuck and exacerbates the lack of fulfillment.

It contributes to an unhealthy environment. When you begin to work on and balance your chakras, the feelings of being stuck and unfulfilled should begin to fade. Once your chakras are aligned, you can look at options from a different angle, perhaps deciding to return to school or exploring more desirable employment opportunities that feed your passions.

Chakra healing can alter your emotional state as well as your thought patterns. This emphasizes the importance of the chakras in terms of health and wellness.

You can use any of the crystal healing methods discussed in other chapters to balance the chakras with crystals. Among these methods are:

- Crystal Grids for Meditation

- Applying crystals to the body

- Crystals carried or worn

- Elixirs of crystal

You can also place a crystal in a specific location to help it balance your chakras. If you are feeling dispassionate at work, keeping an amber crystal at your desk can help you balance the sacral chakra and reignite your passions. Keeping a crystal in a fixed location where you feel a particular emotion can help to ensure that the appropriate energies are balanced.

Crystals can be used for a variety of healing purposes. Understanding the chakras and how crystals can be used to balance them will help you use crystals more effectively on yourself and with others.

CHAPTER 4

How to Increase Crystal Power

"Awareness is the first step toward change."
The second step is to accept."

There are numerous applications for crystals in health, wellness, and daily life. Previous chapters discussed the use of crystals as healing tools. They have covered the specifics of crystal-based healing sessions that are propelled by crystal power. There are other ways to harness the power of crystals and use them in your daily life.

While these methods can help you heal and improve your lifestyle, they can also be used in everyday life to achieve more specific goals and desires. These crystals will become more passive once activated, but you can use them for pretty much anything that will benefit yourself, your environment, or others, with their permission.

This chapter will go over:

- Crystals for Cleaning

- Preparing a Healing Space with Crystals

The tools you will learn in the following sections will help you understand crystals and your power better. You will also be given exercises and methods for maintaining your crystals' top resonating vibration.

Crystals are an energetic tool that has been formed naturally. They, like any other tool, must be handled with care. This treatment includes both care and use. When you know how to properly care for your crystals, they will begin to work for and with you much more effectively.

Because crystals are natural objects, they have their own spirit or energy. They are, in some ways, their own entities.

Crystals have their own vibration and resonance, which gives them their own mind and will. You should bond with a crystal and allow your energies to align before working with it.

When you receive a new crystal, it is critical that you spend some time bonding with it. Each crystal you add to your collection must align with your personal energy in order for you to work well together. The bonding process is what links you to the crystal as a healing and balancing tool.

When bonding with a crystal, you should bond one on one. In other words, you should only bond with one crystal at a time. This will ensure that there are no other external influences or competing energies as the two of you get to know each other. This step is critical, especially if you intend to use your crystals to heal others.

The energetic bond keeps them connected to you even when you are working on someone else. Consider the crystals to be another type of object in your home. Maybe you have a favorite hairbrush or tea cup or coffee mug. You have an emotional connection to those objects.

Whether you like it because of the color, the way it feels in your hand, or the size, you have formed an energetic bond with it.

Drinking coffee from a different mug may feel wrong or disloyal. If your hairbrush breaks, you might try to find one that looks exactly like it because you were emotionally attached to it.

Your crystals will form a connection with you, and it is best to nurture that connection before using them for healing or balancing sessions.

Crystals for Cleaning

Crystals are excellent at absorbing and storing energy. This is one of the primary characteristics that contribute to their effectiveness in healing and energetic work. Unfortunately, this also means they can become engulfed in 'energetic junk.'

Energetic junk is energy that is negative, unnecessary, old, or unwanted and is absorbed by the crystal. The energy is stored in the crystal whether it is absorbed from you, a room, a client, a pet, or your car. As the crystal fills up with energetic garbage, it loses its effectiveness and capacity to store more.

Consider a hard drive in a computer. Every time you transfer photos from your camera to your computer, your hard drive fills up a little more. Your hard drive will eventually fill up with pictures if you never sort through them, delete some, print some, or otherwise organize them. Those images do not organize or delete themselves.

This is what a crystal does. It holds that energy and stores it in the same way that a computer hard drive does. You'll most likely have favorite crystals that you enjoy using. Because they are used more frequently, these crystals will fill up with energetic junk much faster. You'll need to clear your crystals to keep them healing and balancing at a high level.

The good news is that you will be able to clear and cleanse your crystals using items you already have around the house as well as items you can easily find outside.

Clearing or cleansing a crystal is the process of removing energetic junk, or stored and absorbed energy, from a crystal so that it can be used to heal again. Cleaning and clearing a crystal does not imply that you are releasing negative energies into the environment. Clearing the crystal will transform the energy that has been stored in the crystal and then release it into the universe as positive or harmless energy.

Setting the crystals outside in the sun for several hours or under the light of a moon, especially a full moon, is the simplest method for cleansing or clearing a crystal. You can also place the crystals in a window that receives several hours of direct sunlight or moonlight.

When using the sun to cleanse crystals, keep in mind that some crystals change in the sun and heat. Too much direct sunlight can damage quartz crystals. When exposed to too much direct heat, they can discolor or even melt slightly. Before using this method, it is important to understand which crystals should not be exposed to direct or intense sunlight.

Running crystals underwater is another popular and simple way to clear and cleanse them. Take them to the beach and immerse them in the salt water. You can bring them to a lake or river and submerge them there. You can also run them under running water. When using water to cleanse crystals, filtered water, rainwater, and natural water sources are ideal. In a pinch, however, tap water will suffice.

Because both water and salt have to purify properties on their own, salt water is a powerful cleanser.

Water should be used with caution because certain crystals, such as selenite and topaz, can dissolve or become less stable in water. Water is still one of the simplest and most popular ways to clean crystals.

Other crystals can also be used to clear a crystal. Rock salt is a cheap and popular crystal that can be used to cleanse others.

Fill a dish with rock salt crystals, then bury another crystal in the salt to clear it of energy. Rock salt is a very powerful purifier that, like water, can self-purify.

Crystal clusters can also be used to cleanse other crystals. Setting a crystal inside another crystal cluster will aid in the transformation and extraction of energies. However, not all crystals can be cleansed by a crystal cluster. Before using this method, make sure you understand which crystals can and cannot be cleaned in a cluster.

Reiki energy can be used to clear crystals. If you have Reiki level I or II attunement, you can use Reiki and Reiki symbols to clear unwanted energies from crystals.

Crystals can also be cleared by passing them through the smoke of incense or a smudge stick. Other types of energy work can also be used to cleanse and clear crystals.

As you experiment, you will discover your preferred cleansing and clearing methods. Perhaps you've already read one that speaks to you. If not, experiment with a few and see what feels right.

You may need to modify your methods based on the crystals you prefer. While crystals do not need to be cleaned after each use, your intuition will help you determine how frequently to do so. If you use crystals to heal others, you should definitely clear them in between sessions. Combining the energies of multiple people can be perplexing and complicated.

If it was a heavy session, you may feel the need to cleanse the crystals after one session. Sometimes you can use them a few times before they need to be cleaned.

Having a bowl of water in the room to dip a crystal in while performing a session on someone else isn't necessarily a bad idea. Some sessions can be intense, and you may end up draining a lot of energy from a single client. Clearing the crystal periodically during the session can help the session run smoothly.

Allow your intuition to guide you on how frequently you should cleanse your crystals, especially if you decide to cleanse them in the middle of a session. You'll get the hang of it. When you hold crystals that are full of energetic garbage, they may feel heavier or thicker. You might have difficulty using them or keep passing them over for sessions.

When working with crystals, cleansing is essential. Maintaining your crystals is similar to maintaining your car.

Crystal Programming

Crystals are naturally intuitive. They tend to balance and use the energy that is needed without direct focus when used for healing and energy work. Using healing methods such as crystal grids and placing crystals on specific parts of the body are known to increase the potency of the crystal for a specific purpose.

Another way to focus crystal energy and direct it toward a specific goal or desire is to program them. You can program any crystal for any purpose; however, using a crystal whose properties correspond to your focus or goal will increase its effectiveness.

When you program a crystal, you are essentially telling the crystal what to do. This programming isn't just for balancing chakras or healing physical or emotional pain. You could program a crystal to want to get a new job. In order to attract a new romantic partner, program a crystal.

Not every aspect of health and wellness involves the body, mind, spirit, or emotions. Healthy relationships, workplace environments, and home environments are all important.

Crystals not only balance energy, but they can also attract it. They can also repel energy and form a protective barrier if you feel unsafe or want to repel people or things from your life.

When a crystal is programmed, it can be used in conjunction with other crystal healing methods. You can program your crystal grid's master crystal. You can program a crystal to be carried with you. Crystals that you place on your body can also be programmed. You can program a crystal and leave it in a fixed location to do its work.

Intentions should be guided by the crystal's natural properties in order to produce the most effective results. A lot of crystal work is passive, simply allowing the crystals to do their thing. Programming crystals is a more active, hands-on method of working with them.

The steps for programming are as follows:

1. **Clear out your crystal.**

Clear your crystal using whatever method of cleansing resonates with you.

2. **Locate a location where you can program your crystal.**

You should look for a quiet place where you can be alone with your crystal. You should create a relaxing environment. Perhaps with some soothing music or incense.

3. **Hold your crystal in both of your hands.**

To program the crystal, cup it in both of your palms and place it on your third eye chakra. Your third eye chakra is your consciousness and insight center. It is the source of programming power. Concentrate your attention on the crystal.

4. **Set up your crystal**

With your full attention on the crystal and keeping it on your third eye chakra, say aloud a phrase that will program the crystal with your intent.

To program a crystal, say one of the following phrases:

"I intend to program this crystal for... (state your purpose, desire, or goal)"

"Crystal, please help me with... (insert purpose, desire, or goal)"

"I programmed this crystal for... (insert purpose, desire, or goal)"

You can repeat the phrase several times to truly encode the programming into the energetic vibration of the crystal.

Once programmed, you can carry the crystal on your person or in a purse or backpack. It can be worn as jewelry. You can use the crystal in a crystal grid or in another type of crystal healing session.

Crystals can be reprogrammed. A crystal can be reprogrammed for the same or a different purpose.

After you've used a programmed crystal, or if you decide to program the crystal for another purpose, you should cleanse it between uses.

When combined with other forms of healing, such as Reiki energy work or polarity therapy, programmed crystals have a powerful effect.

The only difference between using an unprogrammed crystal and a programmed crystal is that the programmed crystal allows for a more laser-like focus on a desire or goal. Programming is not required.

Crystals function perfectly well without it. However, it is another way to maximize your use of crystals.

Creating a Healing Environment

When you're performing healing sessions for yourself or others, you'll want to have a dedicated space to do so. This will aid in maximizing the healing power of your crystals.

If you only use crystals for personal healing, creating an intentional space to heal yourself is simple. It can be a corner of your bedroom with a table and a comfortable chair for you to sit in. Maybe you'll add some candles and incense as well.

This personal space should be located away from the noisiest and most crowded areas of your home. It should be a place where you can spend long periods of time alone and feel comfortable and relaxed. Perhaps you'll have an incense burner and burn some herbal incense before or during healing sessions.

You can personalize the space by adding images and symbols that contribute to the relaxing and healing vibration of your intended healing space. This is where you can keep a journal of your healing experiences. It is recommended that you limit the number of electronics and technology in your healing space. Too many electromagnetic frequencies, including crystal energy, can counteract or interfere with one another.

If you decide to offer crystal healing services to clients, having a dedicated office space is essential. Whether you work from home or rent a space, you'll need a massage table for your clients to lie down on and get comfortable.

Massage tables are ergonomically designed with a face cradle so that your clients can lie face up or face down while you work on them. Sheets, a blanket, and face cradle covers are required. Additional pillows or a bolster may be required for under the knees or ankles.

When clients come to you in a professional setting, you'll want to make sure they have everything they need to feel at ease during their healing session.

The room should be decorated and set up in a way that promotes comfort and relaxation. Providing calming music, the ability to adjust the temperature for comfort and other details that will ensure they are relaxed and ready for healing will improve their experience.

You should clear the entire area before meeting with a client. You can use crystals or other cleansing methods to clear the space. Depending on how many clients you have, you may not have time to clean the space between them. If you can, do so; if not, cleaning the space at the start and end of the day should suffice.

Cleaning the space is necessary because as you heal clients, their energies can be released into the room you are working in. Often, energies become trapped in corners or on objects in the room. You'll want to clear those energies out so that future clients and you don't unintentionally pick up on them.

Avoiding strong scents and smells in your healing space is one of several considerations when working with clients professionally. Some people are allergic to certain scents, while others are irritated by strong scents. It is not recommended to burn incense, smudge, or diffuse essential oils for these reasons.

The strong scents permeate your entire body. You can get pretty close to them during healing sessions, leaning over them, even touching them if you use crystals on their body or Reiki energy healing. Avoid wearing strongly scented perfumes and lotions, and maintain good personal hygiene.

Sessions will run more smoothly if you have a prepared healing space for yourself and your clients. It will also increase the power of the crystals because the space will be cleared on a regular basis and will resonate with the energies of that space.

It will ensure that you have a professional setting to see clients in, and if you want to make crystal healing a business, a designated healing space will help you do so much more effectively.

The ways in which you maximize the use of your crystals and their power will differ. Use your intuition to determine which uses and applications of your crystals are most appealing to you. Using crystals will empower you and assist you in changing your life in the direction you desire.

CHAPTER 5

Mind, Heart, and Soul Crystals

"Every one of us carries the seed
of mindfulness within us."
"Practice means cultivating it."

NHAT HANH, THICH

The mind is afflicted by a variety of ailments. These can manifest as mental illnesses such as depression or schizophrenia. They can also appear emotionally, as in anxiety or PTSD. Many of these ailments can interfere with daily life.

Mental illness and mental disorders can be among the most debilitating ailments that people face. Unlike physical illness or injury, which can be treated with an antibiotic or a cast on the arm, mental disorders do not always have such simple treatments and therapies.

Most mental illnesses necessitate years of psychotherapy to dissect and address the underlying trauma. During that time, mental illness sufferers are plagued by symptoms and relapses. Many people who are suffering from mental illnesses are unsure of how or where to seek help. Many end up taking antidepressants and antipsychotics for the rest of their lives.

Mental illness can be fatal if left untreated and unchecked. Some mental illnesses cause self-destructive behavior and suicidal thoughts. Others can result in death due to starvation. Some mental illnesses, such as ADD/ADHD and schizophrenia, are lifelong struggles.

Despite the fact that mental illness is very serious and severe, there are crystals that can alleviate the symptoms. Crystals can aid in the promotion of healing and health. They can be used in tandem with psychiatric and psychotherapy treatments.

While crystals can help with symptoms, trauma recovery, and mental illness treatment, please keep in mind that crystal healing is not a replacement for medical treatment or professional therapies.

Depression is a mental disorder.

Clinical depression is a chemically imbalanced state in which the person is constantly depressed and loses interest in activities and motivation. This lack of interest and motivation can sometimes be so severe that depressed people attempt suicide.

Crystals can be used to alleviate depression symptoms. They can also be used to lift one's spirits and rekindle one's interests and motivations.

Citrine, sunstone, smoky quartz, rose quartz, angel aura, carnelian, and amethyst are some crystals that can help with depression.

Anxiety Illness

Anxiety is characterized by a strong, persistent, and excessive fear of certain aspects of daily life and situations. Anxiety can cause an increase in heart rate, labored breathing, sweating, or a sudden and intense onset of fatigue. Social situations, being around dogs, being yelled at, being around guns, and so on can all trigger anxiety.

Some anxiety is normal, while others can be debilitating and crippling. Anxiety can cause panic attacks and, in severe cases, phobias.

Lepidolite, jet, danburite, shungite, black tourmaline, fluorite, and Angelite are some crystals that can be used to help with anxiety.

PTSD (Post Traumatic Stress Disorder) (Post Traumatic Stress Disorder)

PTSD is a condition caused by experiencing or witnessing a traumatic event. The mind does not recover from the trauma, which causes problems in daily life. Nightmares, flashbacks, avoidance of specific situations, anxiety, heightened reactions, and depression is all possible symptoms.

PTSD can be extremely difficult to recover from and live with. Complex PTSD is a type of PTSD caused by repeated exposure to traumatic events as a child, such as emotional and verbal abuse. With additional symptoms, it can be just as debilitating.

Clear quartz, amethyst, bloodstone, kyanite, selenite, and rose quartz are some crystals that can help with the treatment and recovery of PTSD.

Schizophrenia

Schizophrenia is a mental disorder in which the mind is unable to think, feel, or behave clearly or rationally. Schizophrenia is caused by a combination of genetics, environmental factors, and brain chemistry. It frequently leads to out-of-body experiences and thoughts, such as hallucinations, disorganized speech, and difficulty concentrating and remembering.

While schizophrenia is not curable and can be difficult to live with, most cases can be managed and treated with a combination of medications, psychotherapy, and specialty care services.

That doesn't mean crystals can't help with schizophrenia symptoms and treatment.

Lepidolite, ruby, emerald, sugilite, and tiger's eye are some crystals that can help with schizophrenia.

Bipolar Illness

Manic-depressive disorder is another name for bipolar disorder. It causes up and down periods that alternate between manic and depressive episodes. Manic episodes can last days, weeks, or months and are characterized by feelings of constant energy, insomnia, and disconnection from reality. Depressive episodes can last for days, weeks, or even months. Symptoms of lethargy, lack of motivation, and loss of interest in activities become overwhelming during a depressive episode.

Another disorder that may necessitate lifelong treatment with medication and psychotherapy is bipolar disorder.

Bipolar disorder can benefit from the use of crystals. Some crystals are beneficial during manic states, while others are beneficial during depressive states. Some crystals are excellent at balancing both.

Lepidolite, quartz and kunzite are crystals that can help with bipolar disorder.

Dementia

Dementia is an incurable degenerative neurological disease. It can cause memory loss, loss of motor skills and function, and confusion, which can lead to distress and anxiety.

Because it is degenerative, there is no cure, and while treatments can slow the progression of degeneration and alleviate symptoms, it is a very difficult disease to combat and live with.

Dementia symptoms can be alleviated by using crystals like chalcedony, rhodonite, moss agate, lepidolite, rose quartz and rutilated quartz.

OCD (Obsessive Compulsive Disorder) (Obsessive Compulsive Disorder)

OCD is a mental disorder characterized by obsessive thoughts that lead to repetitive patterns and behaviors. Obsessive thoughts are frequently associated with fears and anxieties, which lead to behaviors designed to alleviate those fears.

The most common treatments for OCD are medications and therapy.

Ametrine, amethyst, fluorite, lepidolite, calcite, red jasper, ruby, black obsidian, hematite, and moldavite are some crystals that can help with OCD and relieve symptoms.

Phobias A phobia is a type of anxiety disorder that causes an irrational fear of something that poses no real danger. Phobias can cause panic attacks, avoidance of activities and situations, and irrational compulsions in addition to normal fear or discomfort. The fear of entering open or crowded spaces is known as agoraphobia. It can become so severe that agoraphobics confine themselves to their homes for years at a time. Arachnophobia, or the fear of spiders, and claustrophobia, or the fear of being trapped, are two other common phobias.

Phobias are typically treated with talk therapies and, in some cases, medication. The severity of phobias also varies.

Moss agate, amazonite, azurite, magnesite, labradorite, charoite, and smoky quartz are some crystals that can help with phobia symptoms.

Anorexia

Anorexia is an eating disorder that causes an obsession with weight and what is eaten. Anxiety about gaining weight is caused by body image anxiety. The most common symptoms of anorexia are maintaining a lower-than-average weight through excessive exercise and starvation. If left untreated, anorexia can be fatal.

In severe cases, medical treatment is required to restore proper weight. Talk therapy is used to help resolve psychological trauma and restore self-esteem.

Calcite, lepidolite, malachite, rose quartz, and topaz is crystals that can help with anorexia.

Bulimia

Bulimia is a severe eating disorder in which a person binges on large amounts of food and then purges through vomiting or other extreme methods to avoid gaining weight. Bulimia can be fatal if left untreated. Excessive exercise and fasting periods between binges are two other extreme measures in addition to purging.

Bulimia treatment options include nutrition education, talk therapy, and medication.

Citrine, gold, rose quartz, and tiger's eye is some crystals that can help with bulimia symptoms and treatments.

Binge Eating

Binge eating is an eating disorder caused by a complete lack of control. Binge eating is defined as the consumption of large amounts of food in a single sitting. Eating feels out of control, and food fills a voice emotionally and mentally. It is the inability to control the amount of food consumed.

Binge eating treatments include talk therapy and nutrition counseling.

Crystals that can help with binge eating include apatite, citrine, rose quartz, and sunstone.

ADD/ADHD (Attention Deficit/Hyperactivity Disorder)

ADD is a chronic disorder that causes difficulty paying attention and being impulsive. ADHD is a chronic condition with a hyperactive component. This hyperactivity can be either physical or mental.

Both disorders can contribute to low self-esteem and begin in childhood and continue into adulthood. Symptoms can include difficulty concentrating and academic difficulties.

Treatments for ADD and ADHD include both talk therapy and medication.

Crystals that can help with ADD and ADHD include amazonite, amethyst, hematite, and lepidolite.

Many crystals are used to treat and relieve a variety of mental disorders. Disorders of the mind can be caused by a common cause, such as a blockage in a chakra. As a result, crystals that treat one of the root causes of those disorders may treat multiple disorders.

Understanding the symptoms of a disorder can help you understand the cause. A disorder caused by a lack of control, for example, may benefit from work on the solar plexus chakra. Knowing the cause and how it relates to the energetic system will help you choose the crystals you'll use to treat such a disorder.

When it comes to the heart, there are numerous physical and emotional ailments that can cause distress, dis-ease, and disruption in daily life.

The heart is a vital organ, and heart health is critical. Throughout society, there is an increase in heart disease, heart attacks, and other potentially fatal heart conditions. These conditions are usually physical in nature, but that doesn't mean they don't have an emotional or energetic basis.

Many of these conditions develop over time as a result of body neglect or a lack of awareness about food and exercise. This causes blocks, which lead to heart disease later in life. Understanding how crystals can help balance energy on a daily basis and then putting that knowledge to use can help prevent the slow buildup of potentially fatal conditions.

Heart Conditions Heartache,

Unfortunately, a broken heart is a relatively common condition. Broken hearts are caused by the loss of a friend or romantic partner in a breakup or falling out. Broken hearts can be extremely emotionally draining. They can cause tears, sadness, and even depression. This ache can sometimes be so intense that you don't want to get out of bed in the morning. Sometimes you sink so deep into sadness that the prospect of meeting new people is agonizing. A broken heart can also lead to rash decisions, rushing into another sexual relationship, or outright denial.

While none of these symptoms appear to be dire or serious, some people experience strong emotions. Negative emotions that are not properly released or are obsessed with become a problem. Repressing emotions causes imbalance. Emotional imbalances can also be caused by not letting go or moving on.

Because heartache is powerful and often feels negative, it is frequently repressed or held onto rather than let go.

Heart-healing crystals include agate, amazonite, amber, amethyst, aquamarine, bloodstone, carnelian, citrine, clear quartz, fluorite, garnet, jade, jasper, kyanite, labradorite, lapis lazuli, moonstone, obsidian, onyx, and rose quartz.

Grief

Grief is a powerful emotion associated with loss. This is not the same as romantic loss. Grief is much more profound and is usually caused by the death of a family member or loved one. Pets dying can cause intense grief.

Losing a friend, loved one, family member, or pet in a final way, such as death, exacerbates grief. Grief manifests itself in stages. The first stage is denial, in which the mind denies what has occurred. The second stage is anger, in which the mind lashes out in response to the loss. The third stage is bargaining, in which the mind tries to make sense of what has happened. When the sadness finally hits, the fourth stage is depression. The fifth stage is acceptance, in which the mind realizes it cannot change what has occurred and accepts the loss as a natural part of life.

These stages can take some time to complete. Some people may require grief counseling to get through it. Losing a child is one of the most traumatic losses, and many parents who have lost a child seek help from outside sources to cope.

Crystals can be used to assist in the grieving process and to keep energies from becoming stuck. If energy is out of balance, it may be difficult for the mind to progress through the stages of grief properly.

Agate, aquamarine, amethyst, emerald, malachite, moonstone, rose quartz, rhodonite, and pink tourmaline are some crystals that can aid in the grieving process.

The murmur of the Heart

A heart murmur occurs when sounds other than the regular heartbeat are present. A heart murmur is caused by an underlying disease or condition. They can also be caused by normal heart activity. Heart valve disease or infection, heart abnormalities, and aortic valve thickening

Different treatments will be available depending on the cause of the heart murmur. There may also be different crystals that can help with a specific root cause.

Rose quartz, emerald, aventurine, red jasper, white pearl, kunzite, carnelian, jade, peridot, ruby, and malachite are some crystals that can help with a heart murmur.

Cardiovascular Disease

Heart disease encompasses a wide range of ailments such as diseased vessels, structural issues, and blood clots. Coronary artery disease, high blood pressure, cardiac arrest, arrhythmia, stroke, and congenital heart disease are the most common types.

Heart disease can lead to heart attacks and a variety of other potentially fatal health issues. Most heart diseases manifest slowly in the body and can be the result of years of imbalanced energy or abuse of the body, such as eating primarily unhealthy foods.

Because there are so many different types of heart disease, treatments and therapies will differ. Taking preventative measures is often the best way to combat such diseases.

When used in daily life, using crystals to help with the energetic balance of health and wellness is a great preventative measure.

Rhodochrosite, rose quartz, pink tourmaline, emerald, green tourmaline, and peridot are crystals that can help with heart disease and heart health.

Romance Attracting

Being in a romantic relationship can be extremely rewarding. Healthy romantic relationships bring happiness, bliss, pleasure, and joy, and they have the potential to grow into something more. Building a future with someone else, starting a family with someone else, and sharing a home with them are all examples of this. You can share your dreams and adventures with one another.

While not having a romantic partner is not a disease or condition, it can be lonely. People enjoy the company of others. People are social creatures, and it is often desirable to seek a long-term or lifelong companion with whom they can share so much.

Using crystals to attract romance allows you to align your energy with that of a potential partner. People's energetic connections are what create that romantic and long-term foundation.

Rose quartz, rhodonite, garnet, jade, emerald, and calcite are crystals that can help you attract romance into your life.

Self-Love/Self-Worth

A healthy heart and mind require self-confidence, self-love, and self-worth. When any of these are lacking, it is easy to feel a lack of personal power. Empowering yourself and rediscovering how to love yourself, feel your own worth, and have confidence in your appearance and decisions will provide you with a sense of fulfillment and fulfillment. This empowerment is critical to your personal health, wellness, and success.

Carnelian, calcite, rose quartz, sunstone, amethyst, and aventurine are crystals that can help with self-love, self-confidence, self-worth, and personal empowerment.

Many crystals for the heart and heart health overlap, as do crystals for the mind. Crystals can help the heart in a variety of ways, including prevention and long-term empowerment, and life changes.

There are several other issues that may arise in relation to energy imbalances when it comes to the soul and spirituality. The soul is still a bit of a mystery. People are only now beginning to comprehend the importance of the soul in defining who we are and how it contributes to personality and the creation of life. The soul is also a link to the universe, energy, and everything else made up of energy.

Because the soul is a part of the body, it is vulnerable to energetic imbalances, illness, and disease. Soul illnesses are usually emotional, but they can also manifest physically.

Spiritual Disconnect Soul Sickness

Spirituality plays an important role in many people's lives. It can take the form of religion, faith, or a strong connection to nature. Spirituality emphasizes the human soul or spirit over physical or material things.

Many people find spirituality to be a motivating factor. It can help you connect with your own spirit and create a sense of wholeness or connection with the world.

You may feel disconnected from your own mind or skin if you experience a spiritual disconnect. You may have difficulty participating in spiritual activities such as attending church or meditating. You might simply feel disconnected from any kind of energetic connection.

When you are spiritually disconnected, you may experience feelings of being lost or directionless. Charoite, amethyst, howlite, clear quartz, selenite, and celestite are crystals that can aid in spiritual connection.

Psychic Skills

Psychic abilities and psychic awareness can be intense, perplexing, and strange at times. Premonition dreams, connecting with the spirits of the departed, having a highly developed intuition, being a shaman with shamanic trances, and so on are examples of psychic abilities.

These abilities can manifest themselves at any time. They can be strong right away or take a while to become prevalent. Mastering psychic abilities and learning how to use them can take years.

Having psychic abilities essentially means that your spirit is more connected to the universe than the average person. This connection to universal energy opens your mind to various states, such as different levels of consciousness, trances, visions, and so on.

Everyone has the ability to develop or connect to psychic abilities. That universal connection is possible for all humans.

Amethyst, lapis lazuli, clear quartz, rainbow moonstone, moonstone, and Herkimer diamond are all crystals that can aid in the development of psychic abilities.

Passion

Passion is an essential component of human existence. Unfortunately, for several generations, the concept of passion was stifled by the belief that finishing high school, going to college, earning a degree, and then immediately entering the labor force was the proper way to live life. This mindset stifled the development of personal passions.

Entire generations of people have spent their lives in jobs that they despise. Making a lot of money and saving for retirement so they could enjoy their retirement years became the norm while working themselves to death in a miserable job for forty years or more. The concept of enjoying every day of one's life, including one's job, is a newer one that is being promoted or pursued by younger generations.

Passion is a strong emotional force that ignites the body. Passion fuels excitement, romance, joy, enthusiasm, grief, and all other strong emotions. Without passion, the human body is merely a shell of dull emotions moving through life.

Fortunately, the value of passion and how it should be incorporated into daily life is becoming more widely recognized.

It's terrible to be dispassionate! Nothing is exciting or fulfilling anymore, and everything has become mundane.

Garnet, green jasper, sapphire, red agate, malachite, citrine, and jade are crystals that can ignite, fuel, and rekindle the passion.

Motivation and concentration

Motivation provides you with the energy and drives to begin tasks. Focus allows you to complete tasks. Completing tasks and activities can become increasingly difficult without motivation or focus. This could be work-related or household chores. Throwing in a load of laundry, putting it in the dryer, and folding that laundry may appear to be the most difficult task. Every other little project that comes up can easily overshadow doing the dishes.

A lack of motivation and focus can disrupt daily life, especially if it occurs at work or school.

Crystals can improve motivation and focus. Carnelian, red jasper, rainbow fluorite, and tiger's eye are some crystals that are known to increase motivation and focus.

Creativity

Having creativity allows you to think outside the box. It allows you to choose from a variety of perspectives and angles. Creativity becomes a useful tool in the workplace, the home, and many other areas of life. Even if you aren't a writer, painter, or another type of artist, creativity plays a role in your life.

Perhaps you ran out of room on your clothesline to hang all of the wet laundries. You'll need your imagination to figure out how to hang the rest of the clothes. Even if it does not appear to be a major creative event, you would be surprised how frequently creativity is used on a daily basis.

A lack of creativity can have an impact on daily activities. If you have a job or a hobby that requires a certain amount of creativity but you lack it, you may feel stuck in those areas.

Crystals can stimulate creativity and even aid in brainstorming. Citrine, carnelian, garnet, and tiger's eye are all crystals that can aid in creativity.

You can use any of the crystal healing methods described above whenever you use crystals for heart, mind, or soul ailments, afflictions, or energy blocks. Programming and crystal grids result in a more focused treatment session, but any crystal method will work for balancing energy and working in tandem with other treatments.

Meditations and Crystals

"Paying attention is the best way to capture moments."
This is how we practice mindfulness."

Meditation is an ancient practice that helps to calm the mind, relax the body, and connect the body's energy to the universe. Meditation has both religious and ceremonial origins. Meditation has been used for centuries to help induce altered states of consciousness such as astral travel and trances.

There are numerous ways to meditate, though most practices include some element of mindfulness. Meditation's primary goal is to achieve awareness, attention, and mental clarity on a situation, thought, or activity. It is to train your mind to be emotionally stable and calm.

Meditation has far more applications and benefits than simply practicing emotional stability. The mind can receive answers and clarity to many of life's questions through meditation. Meditation can provide direction and guidance. Meditations can be extremely healing on both an emotional and mental level.

Deeper meditations can transport the mind on amazing journeys and connect it to the universe and energy. It can be a life-changing experience.

When you meditate, you may experience a variety of sensations such as visions, sounds, scents, tastes, and many others. Documenting these visions and sensations is a good idea. The answers or guidance you receive during meditation may not always be clear. Writing them down and then translating the information into thoughts and coherent responses can help you understand what you've seen or experienced.

It can be difficult to find the right groove with meditation if you are new to meditation or have little experience with it. There are some simple exercises you can do to improve your meditation skills. Meditation takes practice, and there are so many different types that you may need to experiment a little before you get the hang of it.

Meditation includes deep breathing exercises. Breathing in through the nose and out through the mouth is typical. For the deepest breaths, breathe in for a shorter period of time than you breathe out. This ensures that your lungs expel all of the air in them with each breath. Only clean, clear air will enter your lungs, purifying your body and allowing you to connect with the universe.

Manifestation is another type of meditation. You can enter a meditative state while keeping the manifestation goal or desire in mind. While maintaining your focus on your intention or desire, you may want to repeat it aloud several times. Using the phrase 'I manifest' at the start of your phrase will help to drive the intention. A manifestation is a powerful tool for altering your environment and your life's path.

Guided meditations are those in which you are guided through meditation by a person or a recording of a person. Their voice and words will aid your visualization and take you on a pre-planned, designated meditation journey. These meditations may have a specific purpose or goal, such as releasing an emotional burden. Other times, they may be to assist you in connecting with a pet or animal. If you are new to meditation, guided meditations are an excellent way to get started. Many are free and can be completed in as little as five minutes.

Group meditations are another type of mediation that can be enjoyable, particularly for people who are new to mediation. Group meditations are frequently guided, but they are not required to be. Being in a relaxed, spiritual setting with a group of like-minded people can be very profound and enlightening.

Meditation retreats are becoming increasingly popular. Whether it's a week-long trip abroad to explore ancient ruins and engage in meditation and personal growth exercises or just a weekend in the woods full of meditation and communing with nature.

Meditation is a type of affirmation. A very short, quick, and powerful meditation is taking a few deep breaths to relax the body and mind and then saying an affirmation statement that begins with 'I affirm.' Many people begin their days or healing sessions with affirmations.

There are many different types of meditation. You can begin with simple meditations and then branch out to try new meditations or more complex meditations. Crystals can also be incorporated into any type of meditation that you can think of or practice. There are also meditations for working with crystals.

The following are some simple meditation exercises:

#1 Meditation Exercise

Seclude yourself in a quiet, relaxing environment where you can sit or lie comfortably for several minutes without being disturbed. Some people prefer to meditate in silence, while others prefer to listen to soft music or a drumming rhythm in the background. Incense or burning candles can sometimes induce a relaxed state of mind with an open mind.

Sit or lie down comfortably once you've created your desired space. If you have a tendency to fall asleep easily when relaxed and lying down, you might want to sit up for your meditation.

Cross-legged with hands on knees, and palms open, is a popular sitting position. Close your eyes and place the tip of your tongue on the roof of your mouth. Begin to breathe deeply through your nose once you are comfortable in either a sitting or lying down position.

Inhale through your nose to the count of four, and exhale through your nose to the count of eight. Repeat the breathing exercise while focusing on your tongue on the roof of your mouth. Allow thoughts and feelings to pass through your mind while keeping your tongue pressed to the roof of your mouth.

Take a deep breath through your mouth and reposition your tongue if your tongue slips because your mind wanders. Then restart the breathing pattern through the nose.

You might only be able to meditate for a few minutes at first. Begin with five minutes, and gradually increase your meditation time each day.

#2 Meditation Exercise

Create a relaxing, calm, and secluded atmosphere. Choose soothing rhythmic music or remain silent. Prepare your environment with candles, incense, or whatever makes you feel relaxed and calm. Make time for yourself to be alone and undisturbed.

Find a comfortable sitting or lying position. If you believe you will fall asleep if you lie down, it may be best to begin in a sitting position. Close your eyes and take a deep, relaxing breath once you're comfortable. Breathe four times through your nose. To the count of eight, exhale through your mouth.

Allow yourself to feel or think about anything that comes to mind, but don't let your mind wander. Once the feeling or thought has passed, return your attention to your breathing, counting the seconds you inhale and exhale.

Begin by meditating for five minutes per day. Once you're comfortable with that amount of time, increase it to ten minutes per day. Increase your time in five-minute increments until you feel ready.

Meditation is more than just calming the emotions and mind. It is all about mindfulness and self-awareness. Sitting alone in a relaxed state and being mindful of what you are thinking, feeling, and how your body is reacting can teach you a lot about yourself.

When you properly meditate, your body enters the parasympathetic nervous system. The 'fight or flight nervous system is the sympathetic nervous system. The parasympathetic nervous system is the nervous system that refreshes and rejuvenates.' Animals in the wild will only enter the sympathetic nervous system if they feel threatened or in danger. The sympathetic nervous system is where the human body spends roughly 70% of its time.

Unfortunately, healing is more difficult in the sympathetic nervous system. Adrenaline and other fight-or-flight hormones are coursing through the body, making it difficult for the body to recover. When the body is at ease enough to devote energy to healing and refreshing, the parasympathetic nervous system is activated.

There are various methods for entering the parasympathetic nervous system; however, meditation has additional benefits that can make it an enjoyable experience.

Furthermore, because healing occurs when the body is in the parasympathetic nervous system, using crystals in meditation can aid in that natural healing process. Meditation can also benefit from the use of crystals.

For example, if you want to pursue a meditative trance or out-of-body experience, holding a crystal, such as amethyst, lapis lazuli, or moonstone in an open palm during meditation will enhance your psychic abilities with crystal energy.

If you feel your root chakra needs some attention, lying down and placing a jet crystal or obsidian stone on your pubic bone, which corresponds to the root chakra, during the meditation will enhance the meditation and provide energetic healing for your root chakra.

If you want a more ritualized meditation with crystals, you can take specific steps to improve your meditation and incorporate crystals into it.

To incorporate crystals into your meditation, follow these steps:

1. **Select your crystal**

A focus is not required for all meditations. Clear quartz, amethyst, and moonstone are examples of generic crystals that can be used to enhance a basic meditation. If you intend to have a focus or intention for your meditation, choose a crystal that corresponds to that intention.

2. **Clear your crystal and program it.**

Cleanse your chosen crystal using whatever method you prefer. Then, using the programming technique described in the previous chapter, program your crystal with the intention of your meditation.

3. **center yourself**

You might want to ground yourself before you meditate so that you can be mindful during your meditation.

Grounding can be accomplished by washing your hands in cool water or by touching or holding a large rock outside. Standing barefoot in the dirt is another effective way to ground yourself.

4. Make your own time and space.

Set aside some time and make space for meditation. Once you've set up your space and gotten comfortable, it's time to begin your meditation with your crystal.

5. Concentrate on the crystal

Clasp the crystal between your palms and form a prayer position with your hands. Close your eyes and begin to take deep breaths. Visualize the crystal's energy surrounding and flowing through you. Visualize your programming's intention and the crystal's energy guiding you to your goal. Sit with your crystal in that energetic space for as long as you feel called to.

6. Session conclusion

Allow yourself as much time as you need to reconnect with your body. Make sure to ground yourself again once you've reconnected with your body and skin. You can keep your programmed crystal until your desire is fulfilled, or you can cleanse it and begin using it again once the meditation is finished.

Reiki meditations such as Gassho exist. This is a type of meditation that is used in conjunction with Reiki energy healing. Gassho translates as "two hands coming together." The goal is to close your eyes and place your palms together. Concentrating your efforts on the tips of your middle fingers. Apply pressure to the tips of your middle fingers to realign your focus whenever your mind or thoughts wander.

This can be a brief or lengthy meditation. Most Reiki students will do it in the morning and at night. It is a mindfulness meditation practice for cultivating gratitude, respect, balance, concentration, and focus. This intention can be held for a few minutes, a few hours, or even a few days. This meditation is practiced by many Reiki practitioners as part of their daily routine. Even if you aren't a Reiki practitioner, this meditation is a great way to practice mindfulness.

If you are a Reiki practitioner, you can use crystals in the Gassho meditation to strengthen your connection to the universe and Reiki. It can also aid in the development of your mindfulness.

Meditation can also assist you in bonding with crystals. It can assist you in exploring their energy and comprehending their crystalline structure. Going on guided crystal meditation journeys is one way to connect with that energy more deeply.

This chapter will conclude with a guided crystal meditation that you can do on your own to increase your mindfulness and connection to energy and the universe.

Transcript of the Crystal Meditation

- All you need for this meditation is a quartz crystal and a quiet, comfortable place where you can be alone and undisturbed for at least twenty minutes.

- Before you begin, you should cleanse your clear quartz.

- Place yourself in a Zen Meditation position. This is a cross-legged sitting position with a straight spine. In the center of the lap, the hands are palm up and folded together.

- For the duration of the meditation, hold the quartz crystal in your palm.

- Begin by taking deep breaths in through the nose and out through the mouth. In and out through the nose and mouth. Inhale four times through the nose and exhale eight times through the mouth.

- Allow your mind to relax and open up to the crystal's energy. Inhale through your nose and exhale through your mouth.

- Allow your attention to shift to the crystal in your palm as your mind relaxes. Allow your mind to investigate the energy of that crystal, visualizing it connecting with your own. Continue to breathe deeply, in through the nose and out through the mouth.

- Maintain your focus on the crystal's energy. It will pulsate, warming your palms and increasing in volume and intensity. Allow your own energy to resonate and vibrate with the crystal's energy.

- When your mind is in sync with the energies of the crystal, imagine it extending a path for you to follow. Consider the path that extends from your feet and straight ahead of you. Feel the earth beneath your feet, and while holding your crystal, imagine yourself walking down the path that the crystal has set for you.

- Follow this path until you reach a white, sandy beach. Feel the warm sand under your feet, hear the waves lapping against the shore, and smell the salty air. Take a moment to absorb all of the details of your beach.

- Consider the ideal ocean beach, with the perfect color of water, the perfect grain of sand, and the perfect size of waves. When you stand on the beach, the weather is perfect, and you feel at peace.

- A boat begins to drift towards you on the horizon. This is a beautiful boat of your design, complete with all the details and luxuries that you can imagine. A boat that represents your inner spirit's dreams and desires. It's far away, but getting closer and closer to the water's edge.

- You are compelled to board the boat when it reaches the shore of your beach. Your feet carry you onto the boat's deck as it gently drifts away from the shore, back out into the gleaming ocean.

- Take a seat on the flat deck at the bow of the boat. Cup your crystal in your hands and breathe deeply in through your nose and out through your mouth to reconnect with the crystal's energy.

- Your boat, which represents your inner spirit's dreams and desires, transports you to a new shore, one you have never seen before. On this beach, you come across a flower growing out of the sand. It's a lovely flower, the most lovely flower you've ever seen.

Everything about it is beautiful, from the shape and color of its petals to the scent it emits.

- Spend as much time as you need in the presence of this flower. Pay attention to any messages it has for you.

- When you feel the need to return to yourself, follow the crystal's guidance back to your boat, across the ocean, and to your ideal beach. Return to the crystal where the path began by walking down the path you took.

- Open your eyes and take a few moments to reconnect with your body and skin. Take as much time as you need before standing up and getting back to moving.

- It is normal to feel dizzy or lightheaded after meditating. Take a moment to ground yourself by washing your hands in cool water or stepping into the dirt barefoot.

- Take the time to record specifics from your meditation. Describe your beach experience in terms of what you saw, felt, smelled, tasted, and heard. Describe your boat and flower as thoroughly as possible. Write down any thoughts or feelings that surfaced for you during the meditation. You might find these details useful in the future.

- Keep the quartz crystal on your person for the rest of the day, then cleanse it again.

Complex meditations can be very powerful and teach you a lot about yourself. They can take you on spiritual journeys as well as deeper into yourself. There are numerous types of meditation that can assist you.

Other healing modalities and meditation benefit greatly from the use of crystals. Energy interacts with energy. When crystal energy is combined with the purest form of your personal energy, such as in meditation, it creates a much different and stronger experience.

If you practice various meditations, you will discover a personal power that you were not aware of. Meditate with crystals to connect with their energies as well as to expand your own. Incorporate crystals into your daily meditation to raise your energetic vibration.

If you are serious about changing your personal vibration and empowering your energetic self, incorporate crystal meditation into your daily routine.

100 Crystals to Know

"Changing a person requires changing his awareness of himself."

MASLOW'S HIERARCHY OF NEEDS

Agate

Agate is a popular crystal found in India, Morocco, the United States, Africa, Brazil, and the Czech Republic. The aura is stabilized by agate. It expels and transforms negative energy. It is an extremely effective cleansing crystal on both the physical and emotional levels. Agate, when placed over the heart, can help to balance the dis-ease in the heart chakra. Agate, when used as an elixir, can stimulate the digestive system and relieve gastritis. It has the ability to heal the stomach, uterus, lymphatic system, and pancreas. Agate strengthens blood vessels and heals skin disorders. Agate comes in a variety of colors, including clear, milky white, blue-green, green, and pink.

Blue Lace Agate is an agate.

Blue Lace Agate is a common stone that is pale or light blue in color with light or dark bands. Blue Lace Agate has a soft, cooling, and calming energy. This crystal works well with the heart chakra and allows for freedom of expression. It allows for the expression of one's thoughts and feelings. It can help with shoulder and neck pain. It can help with thyroid deficiencies as well as throat and lymph infections.

Dendritic Agate (Agate)

A readily available clear, brown, and green crystal. It can be found in the same places as agate, including Iceland. Dendritic Agate is a stone of abundance and fulfillment. If the chakras are out of balance, it is an excellent chakra healer.

Agate: Agate of Fire

Fire Agate is a stone that can be brownish, red or orange, green, or blue. This is a natural stone. The energy is both soothing and nurturing. It becomes a source of comfort during difficult times. This stone is beneficial to the stomach, nervous system, and endocrine system. It also helps with circulatory problems.

Moss Agate is an agate.

Moss Agate can be found in the United States, India, and Australia. Green is the most common color, but it can also be blue, red, yellow, or brown. This is a grounding stone with a natural connection. It is known to refresh the soul and reduce sensitivity to pollutants in the environment. Moss Agate hastens recovery. Moss Agate, when applied to the skin, treats fungal infections and skin infections.

Amazonite

Blue or green stones were discovered in the United States, Canada, Namibia, Austria, Russia, India, Brazil, and Mozambique. It functions as a filtering stone. Microwaves and cellphone waves are absorbed. The stone is very calming and soothing. It has the ability to open the throat and heart chakras. It fosters loving communication.

Amber

Amber is a yellowish or golden-brown stone. It is widely available and can be found in Poland, the United Kingdom, Italy, Russia, Romania, Myanmar, Germany, and Dominica. Amber is a fossilized tree resin that has solidified. It is a strong grounding stone with a strong connection to the earth. Effective healer and cleanser. It has the ability to stimulate the sacral charka. It is said to absorb pain and negativity.

Amethyst

The color of amethyst is purple or lavender. It's a fairly common crystal. A very strong protection stone with a high spiritual vibration. It is an excellent crystal for mental healing. It alleviates physical, emotional, and psychological discomfort. It can aid in the integration of the physical, mental, and emotional bodies.

Angelite

Angelite is a blue and white stone that can have red flecks. It is a simple stone to obtain. It is an awareness stone that represents peace and brotherhood. Angelite unblocks meridians when applied to the feet. It is linked to the throat chakra and can help with throat inflammation.

Apatite

This crystal is available in yellow, green, gray, blue, white, purple, brown, red, and violet. This is an uplifting crystal. It serves as a link between consciousness and matter. Apatite promotes bone healing. It also promotes cell growth.

Aquamarine

A green-blue crystal with readily available color. Aquamarine is a stone of bravery. It has calming energies that help to relieve stress. Defends against pollutants. This stone can be used to relieve swollen glands and heal sore throats. Helps with thyroid issues. It controls hormone production.

Aventurine

Aventurine comes in green, blue, peach, brown, and red varieties and is widely available. A stone of good fortune. Aventurine dispels negative energy. It is beneficial to both the thymus gland and the nervous system.

Aventurine regulates blood pressure, boosts metabolism, and lowers cholesterol.

Azurite

A deep blue crystal that is easily obtained. Azurite aids in the development of psychic and intuitive abilities. Leads the soul to enlightenment. It opens the third eye chakra. Azurite is a throat remedy. Treats arthritis and joint problems as well. It can help to align the spine and heal brain damage.

Beryl

Beryl comes in a variety of colors and is widely available. Beryl teaches you to do only what is necessary. Helps with a stressful life and helps shed unnecessary baggage. Beryl aids in the elimination of waste by the organs. Aids in the development of toxin resistance. Treats the heart, liver, spine, and stomach.

Chrysoberyl: Beryl

Chrysoberyl comes in a variety of yellow hues, as well as brown and green. A crystal that is easily accessible. Alexandrite and Cat's Eye are two more expensive and rare variations of this stone. A new beginnings stone. It activates the crown chakra, increasing spiritual and personal power.

Bloodstone

The color of bloodstone is red and green. It is an easily accessible stone. It is a fantastic blood-cleansing stone. Overall, a strong healer. It has the power to drive away evil and negativity. It stimulates the immune system and lymph flow. Rejuvenates a tired body and mind. Organs are detoxified.

The Boji Stone

is A brownish stone that can occasionally be blue. True Boji Stones are difficult to come by. A very strong grounding stone.

They aid in the healing and release of blockages, the relief of pain, and the regeneration of tissue.

Calcite

Calcite can appear in a variety of colors. It is a fairly common stone. It is an energy cleanser and amplifier stone. Removes the body's stagnant energy. Calcite cleanses the elimination organs. Aids in the absorption of calcium by the bones. Bones and joints are strengthened.

Calcite (Green Calcite):

A mental healing stone that can aid in the dissolution of rigid beliefs. It restores mental balance and aids in the release of things that are familiar and comforting but no longer serve you. It Aids communication in a stale or negative animal farm.

Calcite Color: Orange Calcite

A stone that is both energizing and cleansing. It benefits the lower chakras, the solar plexus, the sacral chakra, and the root chakra. Emotional balance. Removes fear and aids in recovery from depression. Orange calcite dissolves issues and maximizes potential.

Calcite: Calcite (Red)

Red calcite boosts energy, raises emotions to a higher vibration, aids in willpower development, and opens the heart chakra. Red calcite is a crystal that aids in the removal of stagnant energy, such as constipation. Resonates with the root chakra as well.

Carnelian

The most common stone colors are red, orange, pink, and brown. Carnelian helps to ground and anchor the body and mind in the present moment. Restores energy and motivation. Encourages creativity. Other stones are cleansed by Carnelian. It is a vital force that stimulates metabolism. The root chakra is activated. Carnelian stimulates female reproductive organs and boosts fertility.

Celestite

Celestite is found in the colors blue, red, yellow, and white. It is a readily available but costly stone. A teaching stone with a high vibration. It possesses divine energies. A powerful healing force that dissolves pain and attracts love. Aids in the treatment of eye and ear problems.

Chalcedony

Chalcedony is a pink, white, blue, grayish, and red crystal. A typical crystal. Chalcedony is a protective stone. It fosters brotherhood, improves group stability, and aids in telepathy. A purifying stone that promotes the maternal instinct and aids in lactation.

Chlorite

Chlorite is a green substance that is easily obtained. It contains positive healing energy. It is a good stone for the environment as well as the personal energy field. Aids in the removal of toxins from the body and the absorption of vitamins, particularly vitamins A and E.

Chrysocolla

It is a common stone that comes in the colors green, turquoise, and blue. Chrysocolla is a calming crystal. It is a grounding stone that aids in meditation and communication. It removes negative energy from the house. Chrysocolla aids in the treatment of arthritis, muscle spasms, bone disease, and digestive issues.

Cinnabar

Cinnabar is a stone that can be red, brown, or gray. It is widely available but costly. Attracts abundance, boosts persuasiveness and assertiveness and aids in financial success. Cinnabar cleanses the blood. It helps with fertility and weight control.

Citrine

Citrine is a stone that is yellow, brown, and smoky gray. Although natural citrine is uncommon, heat-treated amethyst is sold as citrine. A powerful cleanser and regenerator. The sun's power is carried. It is a recharging and energizing stone. Degenerative disease is reversed.

Diamond

Diamonds come in a variety of colors, including clear, white, blue, brown, yellow, and pink. They are pricey. Diamonds represent purity. They use love to cement relationships. Diamonds are used to treat vision problems such as glaucoma. It also benefits the brain and alleviates allergies.

Emerald

Emeralds are green and readily available when unpolished. A stone of inspiration that represents infinite patience. Emerald aids in the recovery from infections. Aids in the treatment of the sinuses, heart, lungs, muscles, and spine.

Fluorite

Fluorite is a common crystal that comes in a variety of colors. Fluorite is a powerfully protective stone, particularly on a psychic level. It aids in blocking psychic manipulation. Heals infections and ailments. Fluorite is beneficial to the cells, teeth, and bones, and it aids in DNA repair.

Fluorite is a blue fluorite.

Blue fluorite promotes creativity and clear communication. It both calms and revitalizes energy. Helps with problems with the eyes, nose, throat, and ears. Concentrates brain activity.

Green Fluorite Fluorite

Excessive energy is grounded by green fluorite. It heals infections and dispels emotional trauma. Green fluorite is excellent at absorbing negative energy from the environment.

Purple Fluorite Fluorite

Purple fluorite is associated with the chakra of the third eye. It has the ability to open and stimulate it. It improves psychic communication and imparts common sense. Excellent meditation stone. It also helps with bone and bone marrow treatment.

Garnet

Garnet is a common stone that comes in a variety of colors. A regenerating and energizing stone. Garnet purifies and revitalizes the chakras. It cleanses and balances. The body is regenerated. Garnet boosts metabolism and treats spinal and cellular issues.

Hematite

Hematite is a common silver or red stone. It is an extremely powerful grounding stone. It is also a powerful protection stone. Hematite brings harmony to the spirit, body, and mind. Helps with circulatory problems, blood conditions, and kidney support.

Diamond of Herkimer

Herkimer diamonds is transparent. They are widely available but costly. Herkimer diamonds enliven and energize the body and mind. Encourages creativity and is a powerful attunement crystal. Herkimer Diamond cleanses the body and protects against radioactivity.

Howlite

Howlite comes in green, blue, and white hues. Sometimes they are artificially colored. It is a simple crystal to obtain. Howlite is a soothing stone. It helps with sleep. It aids in the balance of calcium levels in the teeth and bones.

Pyrite of Iron

Iron pyrite is a brownish or gold mineral that is widely available. Iron pyrite is an excellent energy shield. Negative energies are blocked. Iron pyrite is used to treat bone and promote cell formation. DNA repair and energetic meridians alignment

Jade

Jade comes in a variety of colors, with some being more common than others. Jade represents tranquillity and purity. It represents wisdom and tranquillity. It is linked to the heart chakra. Jade is beneficial to the kidneys and adrenal glands. It aids in fertility and childbirth.

Blue Jade (Jade)

Blue Jade is calming and promotes reflection. It fosters inner serenity and patience. A steady and slow progress stone. It alleviates feelings of overwhelm.

Brown Jade:

Brown jade is an excellent grounding stone. It is earth-connected and promotes comfort and dependability. Aids in the adjustment to a new environment.

Green Jade:

The most common jade is a green jade. It helps to calm the nervous system and direct passion in constructive directions. It aids in the restoration of dysfunctional relationships.

Jade (Red Jade)

Red jade is a fiery and energizing jade. It is associated with love and letting off steam. Red jade is associated with anger and constructively releasing tension.

White Jade:

White jade is known for its ability to constrict energy. It aids in filtering out distractions. White jade aids in decision-making and outlines pertinent information.

Jasper

Jasper is a common crystal that comes in a variety of colors. It is a powerfully nurturing stone. During stressful times, Jasper sustains and supports emotions. It brings peace. Jasper is beneficial to the circulatory system. It also helps the digestive system and sexual organs.

Blue Jasper Jasper

Blue Jasper can help you connect with the spiritual world. It connects to the throat chakra and balances energy's yin and yang. It aids in the stabilization of the aura. When fasting, aids in energy maintenance. Blue jade aids in the treatment of degenerative diseases.

Green Jasper Jasper

Green jasper heals illness and dispels obsessions. It restores balance to important aspects of your life that have become determinants for others. Green jasper stimulates the heart chakra and aids in the treatment of skin disorders. Aids in the removal of bloating.

Mookaite, Jasper

Also known as Australian Jasper. It restores equilibrium between inner and outer experiences. It promotes the desire for new experiences. It promotes adaptability and diversity. Assists in selecting the best option.

Jasper is a red jasper.

Red Jasper is a mildly stimulating stone. It is a grounding crystal that restores balance in unjust situations. It aids in bringing problems to light before they become too large and negative. Red Jasper brings clarity to difficult situations. Wonderful worry bead.

Jet

Jet is a readily available black stone. It is fossilized wood, but it appears to be coal. It has been used since the Stone Age to draw negative energies out. Also helps to alleviate irrational fears. Migraines and epilepsy are treated. It also helps to treat colds.

Kunzite

Green, pink, yellow, clear, and lilac are some of the colors available. Kunzite is becoming more accessible. A spiritual stone with a calming effect. It has a high vibration. It stimulates the heart chakra and links you to universal love. Kunzite is beneficial to the circulatory system and the heart organ. Aids in the treatment of nervous system disorders.

Kyanite

Kyanite is a blue stone with white, green, pink, yellow, gray, and black inclusions. It is an easily accessible crystal. This crystal is for attunement and meditation. Kyanite has a calming effect. It aids in the treatment of muscular disorders. Also helps with fevers, the thyroid, and the adrenal glands.

Labradorite

Labradorite is a grayish or black stone with blue and yellow inclusions. It is an easily accessible crystal. This crystal has mystical and protective properties.

Labradorite enlightens and connects universal energies. Aids in the treatment of eye and brain disorders. It also aids in stress relief.

The lapis lazuli stone

Lapis Lazuli is a deep blue stone with gold flecks. It is a cheap but difficult-to-obtain crystal. It is a crystal of the third eye that balances the throat chakra. Enlightenment and dream work is stimulated. Lapis Lazuli helps to relieve headaches and migraine pain. It also aids in the treatment of depression.

Larimar

Appearances in blue, green, gray, or red with white. It is a simple crystal to obtain. Larimar is a spiritual stone that opens up new worlds. It contributes to the earth's evolution. Larimar can be used to balance the chakras of the third eye, heart, crown, and solar plexus.

Lepidolite

Lepidolite is a pink or purple crystal. It is simple to obtain and removes electromagnetic pollution. Lepidolite identifies the source of illness. It has a gentle vibration and aids in allergy relief. Natural source of lithium that aids in the treatment of emotional and mental health issues.

Magnesite

Magnesite comes in brown, white, gray, and yellow colors. It is easily accessible. It is an excellent stone for meditation and relaxation. It is a third eye crystal that improves vision. It is high in magnesium and aids the body's absorption of that mineral. It detoxifies the body while also neutralizing body odors.

Magnetite

Magnetite is a stone that can be brownish, black, or grayish. It is magnetic and has a strong positive-to-negative polarity. Magnetite is useful in magnet therapy. It is a stone that aids in healing. Also helpful for asthma and blood disorders. Magnetite calms overactive organs while also stimulating slow or sluggish organs.

Malachite

Malachite is a green stone that is relatively easy to obtain. This is a stone that should be handled with care. It is toxic and should be handled only by trained crystal therapists. Only in its polished form should it be used. It is a versatile healing stone that is especially effective in relieving cramps and assisting with childbirth.

Moldavite

is Dark green in color, it is a rare stone that is widely available but becoming increasingly expensive. Moldavite is thought to have an extraterrestrial origin and was formed when a meteor collided with the earth. Moldavite does not heal individual conditions as much as it raises awareness of the causes of illness.

Moonstone

Moonstone comes in white, yellow, cream, green, and blue. It is a simple crystal that is a stone of new beginnings. It has a strong connection to the moon and intuition. The stone is reflective and draws attention to the moon's waxing and waning phases. Moonstone is beneficial to the reproductive and digestive systems. Helps with fluid retention and degenerative skin conditions.

Muscovite

Pink, gray, green, brown, violet, yellow, white, and red are all available. Muscovite is widely available. It is the most common type of mica and is a mystical stone with angelic associations. Muscovite heightens awareness of one's higher self. It aids in blood sugar control, pancreatic secretion balance, and dehydration.

Obsidian

Obsidian comes in a variety of colors and shapes. Some are rarer than others, and some of the blues and greens are man-made. Obsidian is volcanic glass formed from molten hot lava that cooled too quickly to crystalize. It has a lot of power and works quickly. Obsidian provides insight into the causes of illness. Detoxifies and dissolves impurities. Encourages physical digestion.

Apache Tear, Obsidian

Apache tear is a common black stone. It's kinder than regular black obsidian. It raises and transforms negativity. Excellent for absorbing negative energy. Apache tear aids in the absorption of vitamins C and D as well as the removal of toxins from the body.

Obsidian: Obsidian (Black)

Black obsidian is a creative and powerful stone. It is a spiritual grounding stone. Grounds spiritual energies into the physical plane as well. Black obsidian promotes self-control and connects to the earth. It takes you deep into your subconscious, forcing you to confront your true self.

Blue Obsidian Obsidian

Blue obsidian is beneficial for astral travel and divination. It is associated with the throat chakra and aids in the development of communication skills. Blue obsidian allows healing energy to enter the aura. Aids in the treatment of speech defects, eye problems, and schizophrenia.

Snowflake Obsidian Obsidian

Snowflake obsidian is a white and black obsidian. It is a calming and soothing stone that corresponds to the sacral chakra. Snowflake obsidian is used to treat veins and the skeleton. It boosts circulation. Snowflake obsidian is an excellent elixir for the skin and eyes.

Onyx

Onyx comes in a wide range of colors and is widely available. Onyx provides strength. It offers assistance, particularly in perplexing or difficult situations. Onyx strengthens the teeth. It also benefits the bones, bone marrow, and blood disorders. It also helps with foot problems.

Opal

Opal comes in a variety of colors. Opal gems can be costly, but they are widely available. The fine vibration of opal enhances cosmic consciousness. Psychic visions are induced. Opal increases one's will to live. It is used to treat Parkinson's disease, fevers, and infections. It also regulates insulin and helps with PMS.

Opal Color: Blue Opal

Blue opal is a stone that is emotionally calming. It brings spirituality and spiritual purpose back into alignment. Blue opal is associated with the heart chakra and is said to improve communication. Assists with past life experiences and injuries.

Opal Type: Fire Opal

Personal power is increased by wearing a fire opal. It stimulates the inner fire and serves as a protective stone against danger. Fire opal represents hope. It boosts energy and promotes progress and change. Used to make amends for wrongs and mistreatment. The low abdomen and low back are associated with fire opal.

Opal Color: Green Opal

Green opal is a stone of cleansing and rejuvenation. It promotes emotional recovery and healing. It also helps with relationship connections. Green opal helps to reorient the mind and filter information. Green opal relieves flu symptoms and boosts the immune system.

Peridot

Peridot comes in a variety of green and yellow hues. It is relatively easy to obtain, but good crystals are scarce. It repels evil and serves as an aura protector. Peridot is an excellent cleanser. Toxins are released. Peridot is a tonic stone. It helps to heal and regenerate body tissues. Also good for the skin and metabolism. Helps with the thymus, lungs, gallbladder, and heart chakras.

Quartz

There is many different types of quartz, but clear quarts are the most common. The majority of quartz is common. The most powerful energy amplifier and healing crystal is quartz. It is excellent for clearing energy blockages. Quartz is a master healer and a heal-all stone. It can be used for any condition and has a positive effect on the immune system.

Blue Quartz (Quartz)

Blue quartz can help you reach out to others. It helps to calm the mind and dispels fear. Blue quartz is a symbol of hope and aids in the understanding of spirituality within yourself. It is a beneficial stone for organ healing and bloodstream purification.

Quartz (lithium)

Natural coating and spotting of reddish-lilac purple on lithium quartz. It is a natural antidepressant that can also help with other mental health issues. It soothes anger and grief. Lithium quartz can also heal traumas from previous lives.

Rose Quartz (quartz)

Rose quartz is a pink crystal that is easily obtained. It is the stone of unconditional love and helps to open the heart. Rose quartz is beneficial to the heart. It resonates with the circulatory system, causing impurities to be released.

Rutilated Quartz (Quartz)

It comes in a variety of colors, including clear and smoky. Rutilated quartz is easily accessible. It combines energy and amplifies energetic impulses. Aids in the healing of chronic conditions such as impotency and infertility.

Smokey Quartz

Brownish to blackish in color, with hints of yellow. Smoky quartz is simple to obtain. It is a powerful grounding crystal and anchor. It is linked to the root chakra. Smoky quartz is beneficial for stomach problems, and hip and leg problems.

The Tibetan Quartz

Tibetan quartz appears in the form of single or double terminators with black spot occlusions in the facets. Tibet resonates with this crystal. It is a knowledgeable and ancient crystal. It is a powerful healing crystal that energizes the subtle bodies. It cleanses the physical body's meridians.

Rhodochrosite

Rhodochrosite is a pink-to-orange mineral that is easy to obtain. It is a crystal of selfless love and deep compassion. It broadens your awareness. It filters irritants and aids in the treatment of asthma and other respiratory problems.

Rhodonite

Rhodonite is a pink or red mineral that is easily obtained. Rhodonite helps to balance emotions and fosters love. This crystal is excellent for wound healing and relieving the symptoms of insect bites.

Ruby

Rubies are the color red. They are inexpensive and uncut but can be costly in gemstone form. Rubies are excellent life-giving stones. They energize and balance, but some people may be overstimulated by them.

Rubies detoxify the body, including the blood and lymph, and are used to treat fevers. In addition, they treat infectious diseases.

Sapphire

Sapphires come in blue, green, yellow, black, and purple hues. Some colors are scarce, but the majority are readily available when uncut. It is a stone of knowledge. Sapphires soothe the body's overactive systems. They treat the eyes and regulate the glands and hormones.

Selenite

Selenite comes in a variety of colors, including white, clear, orange, brown, green, and blue. It is relatively easy to obtain and has a very fine energetic vibration. It promotes mental clarity. Selenite helps to align the spine and spinal column. It encourages muscle and joint flexibility. It eliminates mercury poisoning.

Sodalite

Sodalite is a blue mineral that is easily obtained. This crystal bridges the gap between logic and intuition. It also increases spiritual perception. Sodalite aids in the treatment of calcium deficiency. It purifies the lymphatic system as well as the organs.

Sugilite

Suglite appears in the hues of purple, violet, and pink. It can only be found in specialized stores. It is a love stone that symbolizes spiritual love and wisdom. Sugilite is an excellent pain reliever and headache reliever. It is also known to aid in the treatment of epilepsy.

Sulphur

Sulphur is yellow and can be found in specialty stores. It has a negative electrical charge and can absorb negative energies and emotions. Sulfur can treat and heal conditions characterized by flare-ups such as infections, swelling, and fevers.

Sunstone

Sunstone is typically yellow, red, brown, or orange in color. It is a crystal that is easily obtained from specialty shops. Sunstone has a happy energy.

It also improves intuition. Sunstone promotes self-healing and organ harmony.

The Tiger's Eye

Tiger's Eye can be pink, blue, red, or yellow-brown in color. It's a simple crystal that combines earth and sun energies. It has a strong vibration. Tiger's eye promotes night vision and heals the eyes. It also soothes the throat.

Topaz

Topaz is available in golden-yellow, blue, brown, red-pink, clear, and green hues. Red and pink are uncommon, but other colors can be found in specialty stores. Topaz is a soothing and sympathetic stone. It promotes health, aids digestion, and combats anorexia.

Tourmaline

Tourmaline comes in a variety of colors. It is widely available in specialty stores. Tourmaline is a purifier and cleanser. It converts dense energy. Because of the striations on the outside, it is an excellent healing stone. It is a crystal that enhances.

Tourmaline: Tourmaline Black

Black tourmaline is a stone of protection. It shields you from electromagnetic waves and interference. Removes negative energies while connecting with the root chakra.

Green Tourmaline:

Green tourmaline is an excellent healing stone. It promotes compassion by opening the heart chakra. Green tourmaline encourages patience and tenderness, as well as a sense of belonging.

Pink Tourmaline Tourmaline

Pink tourmaline has aphrodisiac properties. It attracts love while also encouraging sexual desire and intimacy. In a romantic relationship, pink tourmaline inspires trust.

Watermelon Tourmaline

Watermelon tourmaline is pink encased within the green. It is a powerful heart chakra activator. It promotes tenderness, love, and friendship by connecting to the highest spiritual self.

Turquois

Turquoise is easily obtained and comes in green, blue, or turquoise. Turquoise is a powerful healer. It provides spiritual comfort. Turquoise strengthens the meridians and subtle energy bodies.

Unakite

Unakite is a green-pink crystal that is relatively easy to obtain. It is a vision stone that brings together spirituality and emotion. Unakite is a healing stone that can help you recover from a major illness. When necessary, it stimulates weight gain.

CHAPTER 8

Choosing Your Crystals

"Start doing what you want to do right now.
We are not living in the afterlife.
We only have this moment, which sparkles like a
star in our hand and melts like a snowflake."

- FRANCIS BACON, SR.

When it comes to starting your own crystal collection, you have a lot of options. When you do begin to build your crystal collection, you will want to look for crystals that resonate with you energetically. Over time, you'll begin to collect a large number of crystals from a variety of sources.

Some people are never interested in crystals until they receive their first crystal from a friend, family member, coworker, or someone else. Crystals are easy to become addicted to because they are powerful, interesting, and entertaining.

It should be a pleasurable experience to amass your crystal collection. You should enjoy yourself.

One of the simplest ways to obtain crystals is to buy them in a retail store or online. Crystals are frequently available for purchase in occult stores, new-age stores, alternative medicine stores, and natural markets. Many crystal shops selling stones and crystals are springing up in cities around the world.

Crystal shops can be among the most energizing retail outlets. For anyone who enjoys crystals, simply walking into a store that sells them can completely change your mood or vibration! Some people are overjoyed to be on a ship with crystals.

It is no surprise that crystals are a thriving online business, given that online shopping has become convenient and accounts for a large percentage of retail items on the market.

Because crystals are becoming more popular, there are a few things to consider when purchasing crystals in stores or online. When an item becomes more popular, many people may try to profit from it. When this occurs, the quality of the merchandise may deteriorate.

This means that synthetic crystals or lab-made crystals are becoming more prevalent on the market. Many people who don't know much about crystals may not even know whether the crystals being sold are real or synthetic. There is much debate about whether synthetic or lab-created crystals are less energetically potent.

From a scientific standpoint, crystals acquire their properties through a natural process. The creation process in the lab is not natural. Synthetic crystals could be a modified substances created to look like real crystals. You can decide whether lab-created and synthetic crystals are objects with which you want to work.

Because this is a potential issue, if you can't tell whether or not a crystal is synthetic on your own, sticking to reputable, knowledgeable crystal vendors is the best way to go. When you buy online, you don't get to touch or hold the crystal beforehand, and it's difficult to tell if the crystal is synthetic.

Going to well-known, reputable crystal stores is a safe bet for genuine, high-quality crystals.

Crystals can be purchased at psychic expos, crystal fairs, and craft shows. These fairs have vendors who rent space, and crystal vendors are common, especially at crystal fairs. At fairs and expos, you can find a wide variety of crystals. Some are raw, while others are fashioned into jewelry or other works of art.

Crystals are available in a variety of shapes and sizes. They can be raw, tumbled, shaped, or carved, and then set into jewelry or art. Raw crystals are preferred by some crystal workers for their work. They avoid cut stones, tumbled stones, and shaped stones. However, the form in which you purchase your crystals is entirely up to you.

The majority of the vendors at these fairs and expos are reputable and sell genuine merchandise. Many of them travel the world collecting and hunting their own crystals.

Talking to people who work with crystals in their natural environment can teach you a lot.

Going to fairs and expos is one of the most educational ways to learn about crystals. It is also an excellent place to acquire new crystals, particularly those that may be difficult to obtain in your area or are more scarce on the market.

If you like crystals and going on adventures, you can look into options for hunting your own crystals. There are many old mines or quarries around the world where you can hike and sift through the deposits in search of crystals. There are numerous locations where you can dig for free crystals. Other places, such as Herkimer Diamonds in New York, charge a fee to gain access to more exclusive crystals.

Perhaps you are the type who enjoys traveling. You can mine for crystals all over the world. This can be time-consuming and costly in and of itself, but it can make for a fun vacation every now and then.

There are numerous ways to obtain crystals. You'll discover what works best for you in your region and on a budget. Crystals can be expensive. The most expensive, flashiest crystal isn't always the best. You should experiment to see which crystals resonate with you the most.

If you are given a crystal, it is usually a universal sign that the crystal should be added to your collection. However, if you are going to buy crystals, take your time in selecting the right ones.

This will be an intuitive process, but crystals will tell you whether or not they are right for you. You may need to hold a crystal in your hands or touch it before deciding if it is right for you. When you pick up the crystal, it may feel warm, or you may experience vibration or electrical shock. If this occurs, it is a sign that the crystal will align with your energy.

Another way to find the right crystal for you is to hover your hands over the crystals. In stores, similar crystals are frequently grouped together in a bin. If you want to find a single lapis lazuli crystal in a bin full of lapis lazuli crystals, try holding your hands over the bin.

A finger may graze across a crystal as you move your hands, or you may feel an energetic pull toward a specific crystal. Close your eyes and use this method occasionally to allow your intuition to truly guide you.

You may not even be looking for a crystal when it catches your eye. That's a good sign that the crystal wants to be yours.

Choosing crystals for your collection is an excellent way to train your intuition. When you find a crystal that feels like it belongs to you, trust yourself and your intuition. It may take some time, but you will eventually learn to trust it.

Purchasing crystals online eliminates the need for that physical component. While your intuition can help you find high-quality merchandise online, most crystal workers prefer to touch and hold the crystals to get a sense of their energy.

When you start performing crystal healing sessions on yourself or others, you'll want to use similar methods for selecting the crystals. Working with chakras may lead to the identification of specific crystals that resonate with each chakra. If you have five crystals that resonate with the solar plexus chakra, use intuition to help you choose which crystal will work best with that chakra for that session.

If you're doing a session and don't have a crystal that corresponds to a specific chakra, ailment, or symptom, clear quartz is your best bet. Clear quartz is a "cure-all" crystal.

When no other suitable crystal is available, it can be used as a substitute.

During sessions, listen to your intuition. You should not choose crystals for a session before meeting with and speaking with your client. The intake period, during which they tell you about their medical history and the reasons they are seeking crystal energy work, will be the primary indicator of which crystals will be used.

You'll have a better understanding of what needs to be worked on and what crystals can be applied to those symptoms after speaking with your client and listening to what they're experiencing. Your intuition will guide you in determining which crystals are best for the session.

You may be drawn to add additional crystals as needed during the session. Don't dismiss that feeling; instead, pay attention to it.

When performing a healing session on yourself, you should have a better idea of which crystals you'll want to use. You should be able to gather them all ahead of time.

When you begin a session on yourself, you may feel compelled to mix it up mid-session by adding other crystals and discontinuing the use of others.

Allow the session to flow with both self-sessions and sessions performed on clients. It should have a natural and smooth feel to it.

Crystal storage is an important aspect of crystal care. You can keep them on display or as decorations around the house. Crystals in a bowl make a lovely table centerpiece. Depending on the size of the crystals, you may need to purchase a stand or a sturdy shelf for them.

Some crystal workers keep healing crystals separate from their personal crystals or everyday crystals. Crystals can be stored in a box with the lid left open.

When there are too many crystals in a small space, it can become crabby and cramped. To keep your crystals happy and functioning properly, try to space them out and avoid stacking too many on top of each other. This is similar to having too many competing energies in the same room. You should be aware of the number of crystals in a single room and what their energies mean to one another.

Crystal storage is important because some crystals should not be exposed to direct sunlight or fluorescent light. Make certain that some crystals are not too close to water sources or in overly humid areas of the house. Selenite and topaz should not be kept in a bathroom where they will be exposed to steam from hot water.

It will take time and practice to develop your intuition with crystals. If you're interested in them and have some experience, that's a great place to start. Over time, you won't have to think as hard about which crystals to use; they will come more naturally and smoothly.

It is important to note that crystals will sometimes leave your life. A crystal can completely vanish and you will never see it again. You might feel compelled to give someone else a crystal. If this occurs, do not fight it. A crystal will usually leave you when it no longer resonates with your energy or when you've got everything you need from it. That doesn't rule out the possibility of it assisting someone else.

The more you become interested in crystals, the more likely it is that your home, apartment, or workspace will begin to fill up with them. If you do end up keeping a lot of crystals in a single room or space, it's a good idea to cleanse the room or space on a regular basis to prevent too much energy from building up. The phrase "too many cooks in the kitchen" also applies to crystals. Too many crystals in a single location can cause energetic disruption.

Fortunately, there are alternatives. You can do it yourself or use a quartz cluster to cleanse the space. Quartz clusters, particularly clear quartz, are an effective purifier and cleanser. A clear quartz crystal cluster in a room full of crystals can help to reduce energy conflict. The same effect can be achieved with a decorative bowl or rock salt.

CHAPTER 9

A Successful Story

"You can't travel on the path unless
you become the path."

The following personal story is about a woman who had a highly intuitive encounter with crystals, which led to her providing much-needed relief to another woman after many years.

She even gives a scientific explanation for why the crystal was so effective in this situation. There are numerous success stories of people who have had incredible encounters with crystals that have literally changed their lives. Whether it is for physical or emotional pain relief.

Others' experiences can be difficult to judge, but there is so much evidence of success with scientific reasoning and personal experiences that it is difficult to ignore these findings!

Personal Experience - Crystal Healing

Kristy Hodges on 06/12/2013

"Obviously, given what I do for a living, I am well aware of crystals' healing power." To me, it's a straightforward scientific fact that anyone can look up.

I was working at a Mind, Body, and Spirit event in Grimsby one weekend. My logical mind told me that exhibiting at this particular event would not be particularly profitable. It would be a long journey, and I'd have to bring my son, who had only returned to school the week before. I decided not to go due to financial constraints as well as my son's return to school. However, my intuition would not go away. I dreamed about the event, people kept asking if I was going, and there was a nagging feeling that it would be important (despite my logical reasons for not going!). So I did.

A lovely mother and daughter came up to the stand early on Saturday morning, and I could see that the mother was having difficulty walking. She appeared to be in a lot of pain. We talked for a while, and the lady was particularly taken with a large piece of Malacholla (a natural, but rare combination of Malachite and Chrysocolla).

This did not surprise me because it contains copper sulfate, a natural anti-inflammatory. Malachite is one of the crystals best known for physical healing. It has the ability to clear energy blocks and neutralize painful areas of the body. When we are in pain, that area of the body emits a high, frantic vibration. Try banging your wrist against something with a really high vibration to feel that 'owwwwww' pain.

The copper element of Malachite causes its vibration to be very low, so we're hoping that by bringing the Malachite close to the source of pain, the low vibration of the Malachite will pull the high vibration of the injury back down to a more normal level, easing the pain!

The lady purchased a small piece and then left to watch the rest of the show. Several hours later, I received an ecstatic and surprising call from my daughter. Her mother was pain-free by the time they arrived home for the first time in many, many years. 'Could it be because of that crystal?' she asked, and all I could say was 'yes,' because I intuitively knew it was. The daughter then took the two buses back to the show to purchase the most significant piece I had in stock as a gift for her mother. At around £85, this wasn't cheap, and even though I know crystals work for many people, it still took my breath away to witness someone else's joy and disbelief... along with their absolute relief that something had finally helped!

I never heard from either my mother or daughter again after that, but I take great comfort in knowing that agreeing to do the show in Grimsby that weekend was the right decision, if only to meet those two lovely ladies. The Universe operates in mysterious ways, and I'm becoming accustomed to doing its bidding. I'll be blogging about Malachite next week because it is one of the best physical healers in the mineral kingdom.

Have a wonderful weekend, Krissy"

CHAPTER 10

Using Crystals to Improve Your Life

"You realize you are not your body; you are everything
when you sit in silence and the wind blows
through you and the sun shines through you."

ANITA KRIZZAN'S FORMAL NAME IS ANITA KRIZZAN.

Crystals can be used daily to boost your energy and vibration. Simply having crystals in your home or carrying them around with you provides an energetic boost. There are other ways to incorporate crystals into your day if you want a more direct approach to including them in your lifestyle but don't want to use them all day actively.

Other ways to incorporate crystals into your life include:

- Water containing crystals

- Bathing water with crystals

- Exercise crystals

You'll most likely discover new ways to incorporate crystals into your life and lifestyle. The more you get and learn about them, the more it will feel natural to incorporate them into your daily routine.

Water containing crystals

Hydration and water consumption are critical to health and wellness. Dehydration causes symptoms such as headaches, lethargy, and dizziness. Dehydration can lead to hospitalization and even death in severe cases.

The human body is composed of approximately 80% water. Water is an essential component of daily life.

Drinking water is the most important type of water. The majority of drinking water is safe, but it is usually treated in some way.

Crystals can help to neutralize the chemicals used to clean your regular tap water. Many companies even sell water bottles with crystal wands that fit into the bottom of the bottle. You can also change the crystal wand.

While putting crystals directly into your water bottles should be avoided, having a crystal lanyard attached to your water bottle can help with the energetic vibration of your drinking water. You can maximize your crystal with drinking water energy shift by using purification crystals.

Even keeping purification crystals near your kitchen sink faucet will help purify the tap water for drinking. Unless you have well water, your tap water is almost certainly treated in some way. If you don't want to invest in expensive water filters and equipment, a purifying crystal near your water faucet can remove chemicals and toxins.

Because water is so essential, the quality of the water you drink is also critical. When it comes to water, crystals have a very powerful vibration. Don't pass up such a fantastic opportunity!

Bath Water Crystals

Baths and bathing are meant to be pleasurable experiences. Everyone takes a bath in some form or another.

If you enjoy baths, dissolved rock salt and Epsom salt crystals in your bathwater have incredible purifying and balancing properties. They are also beneficial to the skin, scalp, and hair.

While it is recommended that you avoid putting crystals directly in the tub for toxicity reasons and to avoid damaging the crystals, there are other ways to imprint a crystal vibration on your bath or shower.

Showers with shelves are common. While filling your back with water, place your desired crystals on the tub's shelves and leave them there while you soak.

If you take showers, place the crystals on the shower shelves for the duration of the shower. Simply being in that vicinity will add an energetic vibration to your bathing experience.

To get some crystal energy into your shower, tie crystals in a washcloth and hang it from your showerhead during your shower.

Maybe you have a job interview that day, so you throw some crystals for motivation, focus, and success into your shower to help carry that vibration with you into the interview.

Perhaps you have a school project that has been causing you stress. For relaxation, focus, and creativity, take a relaxing bath with crystals.

Bathing is a relaxing passive part of your routine that you can enhance by adding crystals. Crystals can change or improve the vibration of any situation.

Exercise Crystals

Movement is an essential component of life. Movement is necessary for the joints, bones, and muscles to remain healthy. Joints become stiff if they are not moved. Muscles begin to atrophy when they are not used. The lymphatic system relies on movement to transport lymph throughout your body.

Movement is critical to one's health and well-being. Unfortunately, many jobs today require hours of stationary standing or sitting. This causes enough fatigue that the body is too exhausted to exercise when not working.

The good news is that movement does not have to be strenuous exercise. Standing up from your desk and walking a lap around the room is an example of movement.

When there are no customers to attend to, movement can be as simple as squats. Movement can be as simple as five-minute stretch breaks during lunch or other breaks during your work shift.

Movement is important, but so is exercise. Exercise maintains the health of the muscles, joints, bones, lymphatic system, cardiovascular system, and respiratory system. Finding the time, energy, and motivation to exercise is one of the most difficult aspects of exercising.

This is where crystals can come in handy. Some crystals can help to motivate the body and mind as well as reenergize the mind and body after a long day.

Getting into an exercise habit, like meditation, will continue to build on that foundation of health and wellness.

Not all exercise consists of a hard workout at the gym, lifting weights, or raising your heart rate as high as possible. Exercise is taking a twenty-minute walk every day. Exercise is dancing around your kitchen to loud music.

Exercise and movement are essential. If you have trouble getting motivated or having the energy to exercise, try some of these crystals:

- Fluorite,

- Quartz,

- Citrine,

- Black Tourmaline

- Sodalite

- Carnelian,

- Moonstone,

- Black Onyx,

- Aquamarine

Any of these crystals can be programmed with the intention of having the energy or time to exercise. You could also keep one in each of your workout pants' pockets. Put on your workout clothes and hold one of the crystals for a few minutes to soak up the energy.

Keeping crystals on her person while exercising can also help you achieve your exercise goals. If muscle tone is your goal, there are crystals for physical strength. If you want to lose weight, there are crystals that can help.

Crystals can provide energy for almost any desire or goal. Crystals are heavy because they are rocks and stones. If you intend to carry crystals with you while exercising, choose smaller crystals whenever possible to avoid weighing you down.

Exercise is another way to incorporate crystals into your daily routine.

What other activities and tasks do you incorporate into your daily schedule? Make a list of the main points of your daily routine, and then make a list of three crystals that you could use to boost the vibration of each of those activities.

Your energy, as well as the energy in your actions and tasks, will shift over time, and you will notice these fulfilling and empowering changes in your life.

The concept of crystal bonding was previously discussed in an earlier chapter. The exercises for crystal bonding vary greatly. You can even create your own if it feels right to you. This chapter will include bonding exercises to assist you in connecting with your crystals. These exercises are excellent places to begin bonding with and working with your crystals.

Creating a bond with your crystals

When you purchase a new crystal, receive a new crystal as a gift, or otherwise acquire a new crystal, you should take the time to bond with it so that it can align with your energies.

You should cleanse the crystal before beginning any bonding exercises. Even if you just bought it from a store, you have no idea how many people touched that crystal in the store. You don't know if it was purchased and returned, or what circumstances led to the crystal being brought to the store.

Because crystals can absorb and store energy, there is a good chance that a newly purchased crystal will still contain energies that do not align with you or were carried over from a previous encounter or experience that the crystal had.

Cleanse your new crystal using whatever method you prefer.

#1 Bonding Exercise

After cleansing your crystal, find a quiet, relaxed place where you won't be disturbed for a few minutes. Place your crystal in your dominant hand and sit comfortably.

For three to five minutes, meditate on the energy of your new crystal and allow your own energy to brush against it. Visualize your energies combining.

After the brief meditation, place the crystal on your third eye chakra and hold it there for a minute. Then, for another minute, move the crystal to your heart chakra and hold it there.

Now, take your crystal in both hands and meditate on it for three to five minutes. Carry the crystal with you for the rest of the day after you finish that brief meditation.

You won't need to cleanse your crystal again after bonding with it unless you want to use it for a specific purpose.

#2 Bonding Exercise

Bring your cleansed crystal to your third eye chakra and hold it there for a minute before going to bed.

After that, place your crystal on your heart chakra and hold it there for a minute.

After you've aligned your crystal with your third eye and heart chakras, quickly touch it to each of the seven chakras, beginning with your crown chakra and working your way down to your root chakra.

After touching the chakras, place the crystal under your pillow and sleep with it there (if the crystal is larger, place it under your bead instead).

To fully bond with your crystal, repeat the above exercise three nights in a row.

3rd Bonding Exercise

Hold your newly cleansed crystal between your palms, palms pressed flat together. Meditate on the energy of the crystal for five to ten minutes.

After the brief meditation, continue to hold your crystal between your palms and place your pointer fingers on your third eye chakra. Maintain this posture and meditate for another three to five minutes.

After you've finished your meditation, take your crystal in your dominant hand and touch it to each of your chakras, beginning with the crown chakra and working your way down to the root chakra.

Now that you have the foundation of how to get started with crystals you are ready to embark on year great healing journey to empower yourself and change your life!

Appendix A

As companion books to Crystals Healing for Beginners there are two other books in this series that make a complete guide to healing, health, and wellness. Crystals, chakras, and Reiki all resonate at complimenting frequencies to each other.

Chakras Healing for Beginners

To read more about the chakras and energetic anatomy make sure to check out this book! The chakras are important to health and wellness. Explore the chakras and how you can use them to change your own life and the environment to live the best life possible. Give yourself the knowledge you need to truly become yourself.

Reiki Healing for Novices

Reiki energy healing is an ancient and distinct type of energy work that works closely with the chakras and also complements crystal healing. This book introduces Reiki and how it can be used to heal yourself and others in everyday life.

Make sure to read the entire series to get all of the information you need to continue your journey toward personal empowerment and a healthy, desirable lifestyle. If you let them, these three books will change your life.

Conclusion

Thank you for reading Crystals Healing for Beginners all the way to the end; we hope it was informative and provided you with all of the tools and knowledge you need to move forward with crystals and empower yourself.

The following step is to begin building your crystal collection and incorporating crystals into your daily life. Building a crystal collection can be a lot of fun. Finding ways to incorporate them into your daily life feeds your creativity and personal power.

You can also use crystals to balance your own energies and even offer healing crystal sessions to clients. This is only a starting point; there is always more to learn about crystals, energy, and healing. In almost every field, practice makes perfect, and crystal healing is no exception. Practice on yourself, your willing friends and family members, and even your pets!

Begin to connect with your intuition, or do meditations and exercises to strengthen your intuition. When working with any type of energy, including crystal energy, this is critical. You will enjoy working with your crystals more if you develop your intuition because you will feel more connected to them.

Finally, if you found this book useful in any way, please leave a review on Amazon! Don't miss the other books in this series, Chakras Healing for Beginners and Reiki Healing for Beginners. The entire series contains everything you need to make an energetic shift in your life and achieve your goals and desires.

Karen.